LOOK FOR ⬚ ⬚ FROM ⬚
FATE

The Best of FATE Series

Psychic Detectives and Psychic Crimes
UFOs and Close Encounters
Psychic Healing and Spiritual Healing: Cases of Miraculous Recoveries
More titles in preparation

The FATE Magazine Library of the Paranormal and the Occult

The World's Strangest True Stories (2015)
True Stories of Strange Mysteries (2015)
True Stories of Strange Psychic Experiences (2015)
True Stories of the Strange and Unknown (2015)
More titles in preparation

THE BEST OF FATE MAGAZINE

TRUE REPORTS
OF THE STRANGE
AND UNKNOWN

ANGELS AND HEAVENLY VISITATIONS

Selected and Arranged by
Phyllis Galde
Jean Marie Stine
and
The Editors of FATE Magazine

Fate Magazine, Inc.
Produced by Digital Parchment Services

ISBN 9781503117037

For information, write:
FATE Magazine, Inc. POB 460, Lakeville MN 55044

DEDICATION

To Phyllis Galde
FATE's own guardian angel

CONTENTS

INTRODUCTION   xi

PART I: ALL ABOUT ANGELS

A Radiance of Angels   14
Rosemary Ellen Guiley

How Angels Made a Comeback   23
John Ronner

Angels or Aliens—Who Are These Mysterious Biblical Beings?   31
Scott Corrales

What do Angels Look Like?   39
Rosemary Ellen Guiley

How I Spoke with the Angels   43
Gustav Gumpert

PART II: ANGELIC ENCOUNTERS OF THE RICH AND/OR FAMOUS

Roy Orbison and the Three Angels   50
Leon Thompson

William Blake, the Man Who Saw (and Talked with) Angels   53
Robert T. Taylor

Clark Gable and the Angel's Advice   61
Dana Howard

Lincoln, Angels and the Emancipation Proclamation   65
Robert M. Webster (Robert A. Palmer)

Angelic Encounters of Paranormal Researchers   67
Brad and Sherry Steiger

PART III: ANGELIC ENCOUNTERS HAPPEN TO EVERYONE

My Experiences with Angels and Other Metaphysical Mysteries   76
Melodee K. Currier

Who Saved Us?   79
Judith Oehler

Where is Our Help?   82
Gwen Beck (As told to Margaret K. Look)

My Healing Angel   85
Charlie R. Brown

The Dog That Disappeared   88
Mai Packwood

Angel in a Pinch   90
Maia Geikie

Angel—With Wings!   96
Raye Wolfe

Frugal Angels?   97
Valenya

The "Money Angel" Who Manifested Just Enough   102
Ellen Marie Blend

Warned by an Angel   103
Catherine Ponder

An Angel's Reassurance   106
Charlie Crouch

Stairway to Heaven: The Story of the Entombed Miners   108
Bill Schmeer

PART IV: GUARDIAN ANGELS

You Have a Guardian Angel   118
G. H. Irwin (Raymond A. Palmer)

Guardian Angels Watch Over Me—And You!   122
W. H. Ziegler

How to See Your Guardian Angel
and Become Attuned to its Advice   125
Dawn C. Athay

How to Talk to Your Guardian Angel   129
Migene Gonzalez-Wippler

What Guardian Angels Want You to Know About Tragic Deaths   137
Olga N. Worrall

What Guardian Angels Want You to Know:
Suicides Aren't Damned—They're Healed   139
Susan Rushing

PART V: GUARDIAN ANGELS AT WORK

The Window That Wouldn't Stay Closed   144
Minnie Alford

Mystery Woman or Guardian Angel?   145
Mary Crawford

The Back 40   146
Martha Sherman

Guardian Angel in the Land of the Czars   148
Eugene Mamtchitch (Translated by Susy Smith)

The Guardian Angel Who Saved the *Essex*   150
Anonymous Crew Member

How a Guardian Angel Saved My Life   157
Boczor Iosif

The Teen Driver and the Guardian Angel   159
Ian P. Harris

The Voice from Nowhere   164
Yves Eriksson

I Hadn't Said a Word—Who Did?   165
Suzan L. Wiener

Notable Contributors   166

INTRODUCTION

THE FIRST discussion of angels and heavenly visitations in FATE magazine appeared in 1948 in issue #1, in the form of a letter from a reader. The second, reprinted in this volume as "You Have a Guardian Angel", was published in our third issue and was written by the magazine's co-founder Raymond A. Palmer under his Robert W. Webster by-line. Palmer was a lifelong mystic who sincerely believed he and others heard the guiding voices of heavenly visitants.

In the more than six decades since then, FATE has printed dozens of reports, articles, and reader letters chronicling the activities and nature of angels in general and guardian angels in particular. Gathered in this volume are some of the most pertinent and informative of those pieces. You will learn more than you thought possible about these eternally busy and helpful beings. You will also learn several ways to contact them, what they want every human being to know, and some the many different ways they have manifested themselves in the lives of people as varied as world-famous entertainers, homemakers, soldiers, and office workers.

After finishing this book, we think doubters will find it harder to disbelieve, and believers will be more attuned to the heavenly presences that are all around us—and indeed frequently hold our lives and souls in their hands.

Sincerely,
Jean Marie Stine
And The Editors of FATE

PART I

ALL ABOUT ANGELS

*I*N ONE SENSE, *angels are like the weather—everybody talks about them but few know what to do about them when they appear. In this section you will find out what modern authorities have to say about angels, how public interest in them peaked just before the start of the new century, some thoughts on what they might be, and even a method for getting in touch with them.*

A RADIANCE OF ANGELS

Rosemary Ellen Guiley
(Dec. 1993)

Rosemary Ellen Guiley is one of the most knowledgeable and prolific figures in the realm of the paranormal and the occult, with over 50 books to her credit, including Dreamspeak: How to Understand the Messages in Your Dreams. *She has studied many forms of alternative healing with the leading practitioners, from bioenergy to dreamwork and past life recall. Here, she offers her own perspective on the origins, history, nature and importance of the mysterious and miraculous beings we call "angels."*

AIMEE S. LACOMBE of Cambria, California, never expected to encounter a real angel. But when she was hospitalized with a rare throat virus, an angel in the form of a woman came to her rescue one night.

The virus caused Lacombe to cough so violently that she would begin to choke. One of these coughing fits seized her in the middle of the night, and was so severe that Lacombe feared she would suffocate. She called for a nurse, but no one came. She began to panic.

Suddenly the door to her room burst open and a short, stocky nurse charged in. The nurse boomed in an authoritative voice, "Close your mouth and breathe through your nose." Lacombe gestured that she could get no air through her nose. The nurse clamped her hand over Lacombe's mouth and shouted, "Breathe!" To Lacombe's surprise, she was able to breathe, and she stopped choking. The nurse said, "Just can't understand why they haven't taught you that." And out she went, as abruptly as she'd come in.

The next morning, Lacombe inquired who the nurse was who had been on night duty, so that she could offer thanks. But when she described the stocky woman, the day nurse looked puzzled and said that description didn't fit anyone on their staff.

Later in the day, the head nurse came into Lacombe's room and asked her to describe the nurse again. Lacombe did so, and the head nurse said there was no one employed there who came close to that description. Lacombe then inquired why no one had ever instructed her how to deal with her violent coughing fits. The nurse had never heard of the remedy given by the mystery nurse.

Lacombe's doctor said he knew about the method. He whispered in Lacombe's ear, "I think you met an angel." Lacombe was already convinced she had.

Lacombe's experience is just one example of the many ways mysterious beings called angels intervene in our lives, often to pull us out of trouble, and sometimes to offer guidance and support in trying times. In recent years, angels seem to be making more and bolder appearances, and are enjoying a resurgence of popularity. More than at any other time in modern history, people are believing in angels, and are talking about their encounters with them.

It wasn't long ago that angels gathered dust, consigned to art and Christmas cards. Except for Catholicism's cult of the guardian angel, most Westerners have scoffed at the idea that angels might be real. Even in the early 1980s, Dutch physician H. C. Moolenburgh found that people laughed at him when he asked if they believed in angels, or had ever encountered an angel. A few people who admitted having encounters with angels were afraid to talk about them out of fear that others would think they were crazy. Undaunted, Moolenburgh wrote *A Handbook of Angels*. A few years later, the book became an international hit.

Similarly, French journalist Georges Huber encountered a great deal of skepticism about angels when he began research for his book, *My Angel Will Go Before You*, published in 1983. Huber virtually apologizes for his interest in angels, in an age where science and technology make them seem hopelessly out-of-date and the stuff of fairy tales.

Despite our orientation to science and machines, the so-called New Age has brought renewed interest in matters of the spirit. We are looking for ways to draw closer to God/Goddess/All That Is. Our Western mythology offers an appealing helper: the angel, whose role is to link the kingdom of earth with the kingdom of heaven. Angels carry the prayers of people to God, and carry out God's will in response.

Origins of the Angel

THE ANGEL is a cross-breed, descended from supernatural entities of Babylonian, Persian, Egyptian, Sumerian, and Greek faiths. Its popular image as a heavenly messenger is generally limited to those monotheistic religions that divide the cosmos into Heaven, Earth, and Hell, requiring couriers to shuttle back and forth between the divisions. This particular brand of angel originated in Persia's Zoroastrian faith and was then handed down to Judaism, Christianity and Islam.

The word angel itself is a mutation of the Greek *angelos,* a translation of the Persian word *angaros,* or "courier." The Hebrew term is *mal'akh,* meaning "messenger" or "envoy."

Supernatural Winged Creatures

IMAGES of supernatural winged creatures have been found in ancient Mesopotamia and Sumeria. The Assyrians had their *karibu* (the source of the word cherubim), which were fierce, winged beasts possessing features both animal and human. The role of the angel as protector can perhaps be traced to these ancestors, which acted as temple guards in Babylon and Sumeria.

The Greeks made a major contribution to angel lore with their gods, such as Hermes, the winged messenger. Hermes is often credited as being the source of archangel Michael. (Many of the Greek gods were molded into angels by the Church in its attempt to convert pagans.) The Greeks also had *daimones,* spirits who came in both good and evil forms, the good ones being protectors. Socrates spoke of his daimon, who constantly whispered in his ear. Daimones evolved into demons in Christianization, and in the process they lost their good-natured brethren.

The Aryans who came to India and Persia around 2500 B.C. believed in *devas* (meaning "shining ones"), who were deities subordinate to their supreme god, Dyeus. Perhaps it was from them that angels inherited their most salient characteristic—the ability to shine, or radiate light. The "el" suffix so common in angels' names is understood in several languages to mean shining or radiant.

The devas made their way into the *Veda,* a collection of early sacred Hindu writings, where they were depicted in a hierarchical (but still polytheistic) arrangement. According to the *Veda,* devas existed in the three worlds—Earth, Heaven and a spiritual realm in between. They were closely aligned with the elements of nature—fire, water, earth and air—which were considered expressions of their existence. Devas of water, for example, were assigned the feminine role of caretakers, or nourishers, of all living things.

Devas also found their way into Zoroastrianism, the religion founded by the prophet Zoroaster (Zarathustra) in sixth-century Persia. It was through Zoroastrianism that vas evolved into angels. In founding this monotheistic faith, Zoroaster rejected the pantheism of the Hindus and offered instead a single, supreme deity, Ahura Mazda, locked in an eternal struggle against his evil enemy Ahaitin.

Mazda is aided in this struggle by the good deeds of humans. He is also aided by seven archangels, the *amesha spenta,* who are the gods of Babylon and Assyria recycled into roles more appropriate to a monotheistic religion.

They represent the concepts of wisdom, truth, immortality, deserved good luck, piety, salvation, and obedience. Each angel also acts as the guardian of something—fire, for example. *Yazatas* are another breed of Zoroastrian angels, and like the devas before them, they rule the elements.

Zoroaster's brand of angels took hold and was handed down to Judaism, Christianity and finally Islam. Islam's *malaika* (again, "messengers") are androgynous beings made of light who act as guardians of humans.

The Appearances of Angels

HOW can we recognize angels? The substance of (or lack of) angels has been much debated through history. Some suggest that angels are naturally occurring energies, and if they seem to us to be visible and have form, then it is because we are seeing them with the inner eye, and projecting onto them a visible form that is entirely subjective.

Saint Thomas Aquinas, whose views on angels continue to influence popular belief, declared that angels are intellect without substance. They are pure thought forms. However, they can take on a physical body if they wish and if it makes their jobs easier.

Modern accounts of angel encounters tend to support Aquinas or the formless energies views. Angels have no standard form or appearance, but take whatever guise seems necessary in order to interact with humans in any given situation. They can appear as human beings of either sex, or be androgynous in appearance. They can be either adults or children. They can even come as animals. Angels also can appear as radiant beings (with or without wings), as balls or pillars of light.

Descriptions of angels have changed over the centuries. Early Bible tales depict angels as wingless and rather earthy and humanoid. The three strangers who enjoyed Abraham's hospitality seemed quite unremarkable, until they returned the favor by making his elderly wife fertile. The man-like angel found sitting inside Christ's tomb was also wingless.

However, in 560 B.C. the prophet Ezekiel had a spectacular close encounter with beings that were certainly not human. These winged creatures descended in a fiery cloud, and had four faces each (one human, one ox, one eagle, and one lion). They moved on wheels and made a tremendous thundering noise. Encounters with angels of this type, particularly those arriving in fiery, wheeled craft, have fueled theories that angels are extra-terrestrials.

Perhaps such encounters are responsible for the radiant qualities that developed in angel imagery. Halos and shining lights began to accompany them by the end of the fourth century. By the eighth century, pagan gods and goddesses were again influencing their image, particularly the winged characters, such as Nike, Eros, and Hermes.

But the fleshiness of angels returned with the rise of the Renaissance. Angels lost much of their ethereal, transparent quality, and became more solid. Some even lost their wings. Cherubs were reduced to chubby babies— Italian *putti*—an image that is still popular today. Angels were increasingly depicted as feminine.

How Angels Come Among Us

THERE are almost as many ways for angels to manifest as there are situations. Most commonly, angels make themselves known through the inner voice, or in visions and dreams, or in the form of mysterious human strangers, or as balls and pillars of light.

Benvenuto Cellini (1500-1571), an Italian goldsmith, sculptor and author, tells in his autobiography, *The Life of Benvenuto Cellini* (published posthumously in 1728), how an angel saved his life in prison. Cellini, a hotheaded man, was constantly engaging in scrapes and fights with other people. On several occasions, he was imprisoned, and was condemned to death. He was absolved once for murder by Pope Paul III.

In 1535, he was jailed in Rome on charges of stealing the jewels of Pope Clement. Cellini was incarcerated high in the towers of the Castel Sant Angelo. He made a daring attempt to escape by scaling down the castle walls on a rope made of bed-sheets tied together. He was captured and thrown in the dungeon.

While in the dungeon, he sank into despair and resolved to kill himself by hanging. Just as he was about to hang himself, a tremendous invisible force knocked him back. An angelic youth appeared to him in a vision and lectured him about the importance of living. Cellini was released from the dungeon on the personal request of a cardinal. He went on to become one of the most celebrated artists of the Renaissance.

Angels appearing as mysterious strangers can be male or female. Most often, they are male—usually a fresh-looking, clean-cut youth. They are invariably well-dressed, polite, and knowledgeable about the crisis at hand.

They speak, though they talk sparingly, and they will even take hold of the people in distress.

Mysterious Stranger Angels

MYSTERIOUS stranger angels appear suddenly when they are needed, and disappear just as suddenly when their job is done. No one knows who they are, or where they come from, or where they go.

One need not be in dire straits to have a mysterious stranger angel appear on the scene, as the following story from Linda Auer of La Grange, Illinois, illustrates:

"I went into a local electronics store with my son, who had his newly purchased shortwave radio. He had been having difficulty receiving certain channels, and believed there was a problem with the radio. We began a discussion with the store manager. My son began to explain the problem, but the manager cut him off, trying to make it sound like my son didn't know how to operate the radio. The more my son tried to object, the more insistent the manager became.

"Suddenly, out of nowhere, this young man appeared at the register where we were standing, and intervened. He had something in his hand to purchase and said very quietly, yet with knowledge, that my son had a point. He proceeded to explain very calmly to the manager what the problem was. Not only did he solve the problem, but suddenly the manager was much nicer. Then the man purchased the item in his hand. It was crystals for a shortwave.

"I was just dumbfounded. The young man wished us a nice day and left the store. A couple of seconds later, I rushed out the door to thank him, but he was gone. He literally disappeared. The store is in the middle of the block, so you would still be able to see someone walking down the sidewalk. Obviously, this was not an ordinary human. I still get chills when I think about it."

The angelic "roadside rescue" happens so often that it is almost a cliché in angel lore. In the roadside rescue, the mysterious stranger arrives to help the motorist stranded on a lonely road at night, or who is injured in an accident in an isolated spot. Or, human beings arrive just in the nick of time.

Angel channeler and author Jane M. Howard, of Upperco, Maryland, is on the road around the world a great deal to lecture and give workshops. The angels have come to her aid a number of times, helping her avert accidents by instructing her on what to do, or taking invisible control of the wheel or pedals.

One night, the gas pedal in Janie's car became stuck, and she ran off the freeway near Baltimore. She stopped the car by throwing the transmission into park. It would not restart, and she began to panic. It was ten P.M. and she was miles from the nearest exit. She prayed to the angels for help, and within minutes, a van pulled up, carrying a man and a woman.

The woman rolled down her window and told Janie not to be frightened, for they were Christians. Even so, many people would have been wary of strangers at night. But the angels gave Janie assurances, and she accepted a ride to a gas station. She discovered that the couple lived in a town near hers, and knew her family. They pulled off to help Janie, they said, because they had a daughter, and they hoped that if their daughter ever was in distress, she, too, would be aided.

Why We Need Angels

WHAT accounts for the new popularity of angels? Why are so many people experiencing angels now?

One major factor is a collective sense of lack of control. Every day, we turn on the radio or television and get a litany of bad news. We feel overwhelmed by pressures and circumstances that seem beyond our influence: drugs, crime, homelessness, economic problems, political and social instability, war, disease, famine, and an increasingly toxic environment. We long for help—some sort of divine intervention that, if it cannot change things on a large scale, can at least brighten our own personal sphere.

Another significant factor in the popularity of angels is that they are an appealing form of divine intervention. Unlike the Judeo-Christian God, who is abstract and has no form or face, angels are personable and beautiful. They are loving, benevolent, wise, patient, and capable of bestowing miracles—or so we perceive them to be (according to Scripture, however, angels will punish humans if that is God's directive.)

We view angels as always with us—they never desert us, no matter how poorly we perform. And even though they do not always save us from catastrophe, they stand ready as a source of strength to help us through all our trials. We seem to have a great, collective hunger for spiritual guidance that is personal and intimate, a hunger that is not being met through conventional religion. Angels are our personal companions, our guides, our protectors.

Also, we in the West are increasingly open to paranormal experience.

Popular interest in the paranormal and things spiritual has gone through cycles in the past. The present interest is part of the New Age, which gained momentum during the 1960s. This openness is part of a collective expansion and uplifting of human consciousness, part of a paradigm shift that is bringing us into greater awareness of what we now call "non-ordinary realities". Angels are helping in this expansion of consciousness by bringing us into contact with higher energies.

Making Sense of Angels

AN ENCOUNTER with an angel does not benefit us unless we can interpret and integrate it—that is, accept it as a real experience. If we are ambivalent about angels, and one manifests to us to rescue us from disaster, we gain nothing beyond the luck of the rescue if it does not alter our beliefs about angels, and in turn our beliefs about ourselves, our souls, and our relationship to God.

We may not get much support from religion concerning angels. The ecclesiastical world varies considerably in its outlook on the subject. Many pastors dismiss angels as literary metaphors.

Nor can we look to science for help. Angels decidedly fall outside the scientific world view.

It is up to each individual to come to his or her own terms about angels. Most important is acceptance. If you have an experience that makes sense only in terms of angelic intervention, accept it as such. Don't deny the experience, or rationalize it.

Angels give us help, either in direct action, or in useful information, inspiration, and reaffirmation of self-worth. They help open up doorways to life, or doorways to other realities—or both. They connect us to the highest and deepest parts of ourselves, to each other, to all things, and to God.

Believing in angels, or thinking about angels, especially if one has had angel encounters, encourages more experiences of the same sort. Philosopher Michael Grosso calls this the "mirror factor of the psychic universe." The psychic universe reflects back to us what we believe, and we then experience what we believe. The stronger our beliefs, the more feedback we get in terms of experiences.

However, we don't have to wait for mundane circumstance to bring the angelic presence into our lives. Everyone possesses the gifts necessary for communing with angels, whether it be through visionary experience, clairaudience or the intuitive voice.

We can ask for angelic help in many ways. Sometimes, we ask for help unconsciously; that is, through our higher self. We can facilitate the interaction with angels by direct invitation, especially through prayer, meditation and visualization. And while we can ask for ourselves, we will achieve far more if we ask angels to help others.

If you are in the habit of praying or meditating, bring angels into your daily awareness. Contemplate their power, and how you can bring this power into your life for good purpose. Expect miracles. They happen.

HOW ANGELS MADE
A COMEBACK

John Ronner
(Dec. 1991)

John Ronner is an internationally recognized authority on heavenly visitations. The author of The Angel Library, *a 500 page compendium of facts, figures, sightings, legend, folklore, angelic names, powers, and much, much more that is the outcome of a lifetime of research. Ronner has appeared on The Learning Channel,* Sightings, *and numerous documentaries and television specials. Below, he chronicles how belief in angels waned with the rise of the materialistic, scientific age, and then returned again in the latter years of the 20th century.*

THEY WERE disbelieved in, ridiculed, and finally ignored for centuries in the rational Western world. But now, there are scattered signs that these "Breaths of God" may be winging their way off the Christmas card covers and back into our belief system. Consider these events:

On the theological front, the Pope's declaration in the mid-1980s that angels literally exist touched off a sharp debate in the Roman Catholic church. The debate drew international news coverage.

On the psychological front, thousands of people have gone public in recent years to talk about near-death experiences and the angel-like "beings of light" they often encountered. Just last year, the book *Closer to the Light,* a pediatrician's account of the near-death experiences of children he interviewed, was featured on the *Oprah Winfrey* TV show. The book drew material from a scientific study by Morse, which was published in 1986 in the *American Journal of Diseases of Children,* the pediatric journal of the American Medical Association.

On the cultural front, a spate of mature, cross-cultural books on the subject of angels has appeared. A recent example of this publishing current is Malcolm Godwin's 1990 *Angels,* which became a well-promoted selection of the prestigious Literary Guild Book Club. Sophy Burnham's *A Book of Angels,* which appeared only in 1990 with an arrestingly beautiful cover, went through nearly a dozen trade paperback printings in short order. Some bookshops now have small, separate angel book sections. In fact, an angel even became the star of a prime-time TV show (discussed below.)

23

On the news front, Dutch surgeon Hans Moolenburgh's random survey of 400 patients in the 1980s turned up the fact that at least eight per cent claimed to have had an angelic encounter. Moolenburgh's findings, reported in his book *A Handbook of Angels,* made big headlines in Holland. Writing in 1986, author Harvey Humann reported in *The Many Faces of Angels* that two of every three young Americans questioned in a Gallup poll acknowledged a belief in angels.

Superior Beings

IN VIEW of all this, it's startling to consider just how far angels had drifted from our awareness in just a few short centuries. In the Middle Ages people were obsessed with the idea of superior spiritual beings. Carved angels crowded the ornamentation of churches. Believers often kept diaries, called *fiorettis,* of times in their lives when angels intervened. The supreme Italian poet, Dante, touched minds deeply all over Europe with his tale of a visit to the highest heavens, swarming with angels.

How Many Angels . . .

SO SERIOUSLY were angels taken that scholars spent significant amounts of time debating angels' finer points. These debates were subtle mind games of logic. "How many angels can stand on the point of a needle?" has become the most famous of these brain teasers, called *quodlibets.*

(Answer: All the angels in God's universe can, since angels, some philosophers felt, have no matter or mass and therefore take up no space.)

Then, in the 1600s, came scientific materialism, a new way of looking at the world that said the physical is all there is. The angels, not verifiable in anybody's laboratory, began a 300-year fall from human acceptance, far longer than Lucifer's fabled nine-day plummet from heaven.

Remarking on the attitude toward angels not so long ago, author Claus Westermann noted, "If we listen carefully to how people speak of angels today, one thing stands out. People don't believe in angels anymore. They haven't believed in angels in centuries."

Materialism Under Attack

BUT THESE DAYS, materialism is under heavy attack on fronts ranging from spreading Eastern mysticism to the bizarre picture of reality emerging from subatomic physics. And the angels seem to be spreading their wings again in a new era of greater spirituality.

In December 1986, the 4.2-million circulation religious magazine *Guideposts* devoted much of its monthly issue to angels. One of the most dramatic articles was a first-person report by Smith College Professor S. Ralph Harlow of his and his wife's breathtaking encounter with dazzling angels.

The incident came as he and his wife strolled through woods in Ballardvale, Massachusetts, in May 1960. Stunned, the couple watched six gloriously beautiful entities pass over their heads, "earnestly conversing with one another before fading out," Harlow wrote.

Meanwhile, angels attracted a weekly prime time TV audience of millions, thanks to former *Bonanza* and *Little House* star, the late Michael Landon. Landon played the human-like angel Jonathan Smith on the show *Highway to Heaven*. Although Smith has supernatural powers, he preferred to coax human beings into solving their own problems by helping each other.

The Pope Speaks

IN JULY 1986 came more good press for the angels. For three weeks, Pope John Paul II lectured thousands of pilgrims on angels. The pontiff created tension between conservative and liberal Catholics by sternly criticizing materialists and rationalists for doubting the existence of angels. He summed up angels as "creatures of spiritual nature endowed with intellects and a free will and superior to man."

Angels appear to be enjoying renewed interest amid a general revival of things metaphysical in modern times, from channeling to mental healing. Although scientific materialism has been slowly fading for decades, one watershed was reached in the mid-1970s with the publication of Raymond Moody's book, *Life After Life*.

The Near-Death Experience

A PSYCHIATRIST, Moody had collected, offhand for years, scores of personal anecdotes of near-death experiences. Moody's collection indicated that persons nearing death often undergo an out-of-body experience. They sometimes achieve an exalted illumination similar to descriptions of cosmic consciousness, and they also frequently meet brilliant "beings of light" who are prepared to escort them to the Beyond or turn them back to the living.

The beings of light are described as shapeless glows with lively personalities that are overwhelmingly loving and compassionate. They even are reported to have a sense of humor.

Some near-death patients have told Moody and other researchers they never wanted to leave the dynamic presence of these beings. The witnesses' descriptions of these luminous personalities at least fit the concept of superior spiritual beings. But how the witnesses actually identify the beings varies according to the observers' cultural background. A Christian might speak of Jesus, a Jew of an angel, and a secular person simply of "a being of light."

The beings often question the dying mortals about their lives on earth. And they frequently show them a panoramic, 3-D flashback of every tiny action in those lives to get an answer to a primary question: How much has the dying person learned to love? Through it all, the being is warmly supportive, pointing out that even the mistakes are learning experiences.

Moody's classic book and the near-death research it sparked have helped bring thousands of purported angel witnesses out of the closet. Some of them had allegedly been contacted by higher powers or simply dead loved ones, but had kept silent before now for fear of ridicule.

A Personal Experience

MY OWN SISTER, Susan Bradford, was one, waiting four years to tell me because another relative had scoffed at her story. Weeks after a favorite aunt of hers died, Susan was still troubled. One night, she said, she awoke with a start and clearly saw the translucent spirit of the aunt at the foot of her bed. The aunt told her not to worry, she was no longer in pain and was now happy. Then, the aunt, wearing the hospital gown she had on the day she died, suddenly disappeared, as Susan told it.

Here the aunt would certainly have been a helpful human spirit and not an angel. In this story, however, she had played the kind of comforting role often claimed for dead loved ones by their survivors. Indeed, this kind of benevolent intervention—and sometimes even a more lasting guardianship—seems to be something done by the departed human spirit, as well as the classic superior spiritual being which we call an angel. For example, near-death survivors have consistently reported seeing both types helping them.

Have You Seen an Angel?

AS EARLY AS 1973, pollsters at the University of Chicago's National Opinion Research Center bluntly asked a representative sampling of 1,467 Americans: "Have you ever felt that you were in contact with someone who died?" Twenty-seven per cent said yes. Among widows and widowers who reported contact with dead spouses, the percentage rose to 51 per cent.

Typical of many modern classic angel reports is author Hope Friedmann's story. Friedmann wrote about how her Angelic wings are mentioned in the Bible, although the earliest Biblical books make no mention of wings, and early artists often showed angels as wingless youths. In later art, wings have symbolized, among other things, the belief that angels, as spiritual beings, move with the rapid speed of thought.

Angels have traditionally been thought of as organized in hierarchies, much as life on earth is hierarchical, from amoeba to man. The least developed angels supposedly guard individual human beings. "Higher" ones look after nations and important leaders. Still higher angels secretly keep the physical laws of the universe operating. The highest angels spend their time contemplating and experiencing God.

This is basically the outlook of the Middle Ages' top Western angel scholar, Thomas Aquinas. Aquinas got these ideas mostly from an ancient writer who called himself Dionysius, apparently so his readers would assume he was an authoritative Christian mentioned in the .New Testament. After some centuries, Christian scholars eventually realized that the real Dionysius had not written the book on angel hierarchies. But by that time, the Church liked the other Dionysius' system. To be frank, the angels' exact organization has always been grist for philosophic argument and sheer speculation. However, Protestant reformer John Calvin perhaps took too harsh a view of it all when he called the classification of angels the vain babblings of idle men.

Aquinas and like-minded philosophers have reasoned that angelic intellect ought to be advanced over ours, growing stronger and stronger as one moves to higher and higher orders. The highest angels, they deduced, should be able to draw a vast number of conclusions from a few simple observations, just as Newton saw more in the legendary falling apple than a chance to eat. While there is no proof of this, it may be worth noting that near-death survivors sometimes report being able to think more clearly and rapidly in their spirit bodies.

Philosophers and Angels

PHILOSOPHERS like Aquinas, John Locke (whose ideas helped inspire the Declaration of Independence), and Gottfried Leibnitz have tried to show with logic alone that angels exist. They note that the

27

visible world is a vast, hierarchical chain of beings from the tiniest creatures up to man. Every conceivable biological rung on the ladder upwards is filled. Is it reasonable, they argue, to assume that the ascending ladder breaks off abruptly with man, as the pinnacle of creation? That would leave a huge gap, a chasm, between man and God.

As supposedly indestructible spirits, angels are generally believed by philosophers to be immortal, although not eternal. That is, an angel will always exist but he was not always here. Only God, who created angels before the physical universe was made, was eternal according to the most common—and unproved—opinion. However, the evidence for an immortal human soul is suggestive on this point. To symbolize angels' immortality, artists often have painted them as youths.

A Swinging Pendulum

IN MODERN TIMES, the pendulum has still not swung back to the near-universal belief in angels or angel-like beings held in ancient times, when a Roman's birthday celebration honored not himself, but his guardian spirit.

Nevertheless, more and more moderns seem to be adopting the attitude of Shakespeare's Hamlet. After seeing the ghost of his murdered father, the young Danish prince turned to his formerly skeptical but now shaken acquaintance Horatio, who had also seen the spirit. Hamlet said, "There are more things in heaven and earth, Horatio, than are dreamt of in your philosophy."

Recommended Angelic Reading

DURING 14 months of research on my first book, *Do You Have A Guardian Angel?*, I was struck by how easy it was to find a book about angels but how hard it was to find one that handled the subject maturely and cross-culturally. To help you, if you are interested in knowing more about angels, here is a short, annotated bibliography of some of the most readable angel volumes. A few of these books are out of print:

Dictionary of Angels by Gustav Davidson. In the area of angel lore, Davidson's reference work, *A Dictionary of Angels* has been a browser's delight for two decades. Davidson, the author-editor of a dozen books, spent 15 years researching this 414-page classic. It includes hundreds of alphabetically arranged angel "biographies" drawn from the Bible and other holy books, literature, folklore, legend and myth. (Macmillan Publishing Co.).

Breaths of God by Emily Hahn. A sweet and whimsical look at the world of angels, written with a light touch. (Doubleday and Co.).

A Book of Angels by Sophy Burnham. This beautifully illustrated book is brimming with fascinating facts and stories. Comprehensive and cross-cultural, it is highly readable. One of my personal favorites. Burnham, by the way, tells how she herself was once rescued from death by an angel. (Ballantine Books).

Do You Have A Guardian Angel? by John Ronner. Now in its fourth printing, the book is a general treatment of the subject of angels in a question-and-answer format and has been favorably reviewed nationally in such media as *Library Journal* and *The Washington Times*. (Mamre Press).

The Many Faces of Angels by Harvey Humann. Humann writes from a metaphysical standpoint and is full of fresh, unconventional thinking. There is a discussion of such things as the connection between angelology and Edgar Cayce, holy ground, and the controversial claim that nature spirits actually exist. A quick, enjoyable read. (DeVorss & Co.).

A Handbook of Angels by H.C. Moolenburgh, M.D. Here is the Judeo-Christian viewpoint on angels. The book leads off with a report on a random survey Moolenburgh conducted of 400 patients to determine the frequency of angelic encounters. This survey's results made big headlines in Moolenburgh's native Holland. (C.W. Daniel).

Angels: Ministers of Grace by Geddes MacGregor. A cosmopolitan book by a well-known religious thinker and writer. Among a variety of things, MacGregor discusses angels in various religions and how angels fit into the idea of evolution. (Paragon House).

The Angels and Us by Mortimer Adler. The famed philosopher writes with a scholarly style. A feast of well-synthesized information from a learned mind. (Macmillan Publishing Co.).

Men and Angels by Theodora Ward. Another one of the more information-rich popular angel books. One bonus here is several sections of classic illustrations on high quality paper. (Viking Press).

Angels: An Endangered Species by Malcolm Godwin. A detailed and delightful voyage into angel lore. There are almost 200 arresting illustrations in this large-format book for the coffee table, the majority of them in full color. The illustrations alone are worth the price of the book. (Simon and Schuster).

ANGELS OR ALIENS—WHO ARE THESE MYSTERIOUS BIBLICAL BEINGS?

Scott Corrales
(Dec. 2000)

What are angels? For millennia they were accepted as created by—or emanations from—an all-powerful Divinity who created the universe. In more modern times, they have been linked with UFOs, other dimensional visitors, paranormal, and even psychological phenomenon. In this essay, Scott Corrales, editor of Inexplicata: The Journal of Hispanic Ufology, *offers one intriguing and mind-stretching hypothesis that is sure to set people thinking.*

"*I SAW WATCHERS in my vision, a dream vision, and behold two of them argued about me . . . and they were engaged in a great quarrel concerning me. I asked them: 'You, why do you argue thus about me?' They answered and said to me: 'We have been made masters and rule over the sons of men.' And they said to me, 'Which of us do you choose? . . .'*"

The preceding is a fragment from the *Testament of Amram*, a document written in Aramaic which forms part of the Qumran scrolls, more commonly known as the Dead Sea Scrolls. The entire fragment, some eight patchy paragraphs, relates a story told by Moses' father, Amram, to his children, concerning the burden of choice: whether to serve the evil Watcher Melkiresha, a viper-faced demon, or his counterpart, the Watcher Melchizedek, who is ruler of the "Sons of Light."

Much has been made over the last few decades of the link between the role played by the Biblical Watchers and that played by UFOs and their occupants, as well as the phenomena associated with them. This order of nonhuman beings, which fell from grace on account of their transgressions with "the daughters of men;" are at the core of a current controversy. The viper-eyed Melkiresha, allegorical though it may be, is strangely reminiscent of some of the more reptilian UFO entities that have been reported in a number of encounters. The Watchers, as described in the Bible or by the Tibetan monks who discussed the topic with the Russian artist/mystic Nicholas Roerich (whose paintings of Asian hill-forts are often referred to in the writings of

H.P. Lovecraft), are in essence a race of beings which have always lived in the skies and lord over humanity, reveling in intermarriage with humans. The Biblical Noah, for example, was the offspring of a Watcher.

Struggles of Angels and Men

MEXICAN AUTHOR Luis Ramirez Reyes describes interaction between the same kind of strange beings and humans taking place in our very own times. While the following report would perhaps be better filed under "alien aggression," there are certain elements which make it a more suitable fit for "interaction between humans and hostile spiritual agencies?"

In 1993, Rafael Perrin, a television talk show personality, was hosting a party one night at his apartment in Mexico City's swank "Zona Rosa" district. Around midnight, he stepped out onto his balcony to catch a breath of fresh air when, looking down to the sidewalk, he noticed a wounded dog lying on the sidewalk, twisting and howling. Moved by the sight, Perrin left his apartment to assist the suffering animal, but was prevented from touching the dog by a "young fellow dressed in rags," who in spite of his reduced circumstances did not act like a beggar. The youth told Perrin that a band of aliens roaming the streets of Mexico City had inflicted harm upon the canine with a small beam-emitting device they carried on them. Perrin was further astonished when the young beggar went into a lengthy discussion of the beam weapon's origin, its effect, the nature of the predatory aliens and the damage attributed to "unknown parties" that was common in the area. The youth was about to heal the suffering dog using a similar device which "reversed the effect" of the harmful beam.

Rather than staying to witness the miraculous cure, Perrin ran back up to his apartment to fetch his camcorder, hoping to capture on film the curing of an injured animal by means of nonhuman technology. But when he returned to the scene, the young beggar was nowhere in sight.

Perrin saw only the no-longer-wounded dog walking away down the sidewalk. "Imagine how I regret not having remained to witness the way in which that person used the device and . .. listening to his accounts of how there were aliens among us, fighting and squabbling with each other over control of the earth."

Readers may take Perrin's story, as told to Ramirez Reyes, with a grain of salt, but note the similarity to Biblical accounts of warring factions of angels (or the mysterious Watchers) and the propensity of angels to appear as young human males, endowed with special powers.

In November 1991, Monica Maria Ortega, a young Colombian woman, told of a nocturnal sexual encounter with an alleged "alien" (which could well have been one of the Watchers) on a nationally syndicated TV show. Far from being one of the current crop of "Greys", her nonhuman lover was more in step with the traditional sky people, elementals, or other creatures who have interacted with humans on a biological level in traditions that span the globe. Ms. Ortega was 12 years old at the time and living in New York City when this tall, blond, green-eyed entity suddenly materialized in her bedroom.

"At first, I saw two lights. I felt a presence, and naturally felt scared. One light was red in color and the other was green," she recalled. The lights told her not to fear for her safety. As she began to fall asleep, in spite of the luminous globes' presence, she felt caresses and kisses all over her body as her nightclothes were removed. "I felt something spread my legs open and a sharp pain soon after. I woke up, terrified, and saw a being in a tight-fitting outfit in bed with me. His eyes were so green that it made me dizzy to look at them. I found him very handsome, was attracted to him and fell in love."

Monica's lover and his silent companion (never manifested in human form) told her that they traveled around the world. Curiosity, they advised her, was the motivation for their sexual contacts.

In 1987, Monica had her third contact with the Watchers. After two years, she had moved back to Colombia, and was overjoyed at seeing her otherworldly lover again. At the end of their encounter, Monica expressed a desire to go with him to "his world," but the being turned her down. Nineteen years old at the time of the interview, the young woman had still not had sex with a human male. "They have the advantage," she explained, meaning the Watchers, "of not making you pregnant."

A History of the Watchers

THE MYSTICAL FIGURE of Apollonius of Tyana—sorcerer, philosopher and indefatigable traveler—visited a place, according to the chronicles, known as the City of the Gods, whose inhabitants allegedly "lived on the earth, yet outside it at the same time." Said parallel universe or dimension was located in the Himalayas, and as Apollonius and his guide, Damis, would near their destination, the more unreal the landscape became. Apollonius' larger-than-life adventures include teleportation away from the court of the Emperor Domitian in A.D. 96, and other occult phenomena.

Could these skills have been learned in the City of the Gods? Considering Apollonius' stature in ancient history, could he himself have been a Watcher?

Metal disks have been reported in the skies over the Himalayas for centuries. These have been considered manifestations of the Watchers by the lamas of Tibet and Nepal—"a sign of Shambhala," the subterranean (or extra-dimensional) land ruled by a higher order of beings who visit our world in gleaming metallic vehicles. Foremost among Shambhala's denizens is the *Rigden-Jye-Po,* the King of the World, who is identified with the leader of the Sons of Light mentioned in the Dead Sea Scrolls.

The Scriptures Speak

TO THE DISMAY of those who expect hard-boiled facts every time, the vast majority of the literature concerning the Watchers lies in mythology and in religious documents such as the Old Testament. In the Apocryphal book which bears his name, the Old Testament figure Enoch is taken to heaven to intercede on behalf of the fallen Watchers with the angels of the highest heavens. The appeal is turned down: for having taught the secrets of nature to human females, and worse yet, for having conceived children with human females (the giant Nephilim), the 200 spirits involved are condemned to never again regain their lofty status.

We are given the names of the ringleaders of this heavenly conspiracy, and one of them, in particular, does more than ring a bell to a ufologically-minded ear: Semyaz. While phonetic similarity proves nothing, it is unusual that the leader of the alleged "Pleiadans" visiting Billy Meier at his Swiss retreat should call herself Semjase. Meier's claims have been at the center of a number of disputes, mainly accusations of fraud concerning the fantastic UFO photographs which he circulated.

What evidence suggests that the Watchers mentioned by the ancient religious chronicles, and the entities that accompany the UFO phenomenon, are one and the same? A careful examination of certain contemporary cases, along with some outstanding ancient ones, can leave no doubt as to the conflict between the fallen Watchers (the 200 which descended in the ancient Middle East, led by Semyaz/Semjase), the "Forces of Good," and hapless mortal humans, stuck squarely in the middle.

Quetzalcoatl—Watcher in the New World?

"BUT LIFE had need of an intelligence to embrace the universe. We cannot provide it, said the Old Ones. It has never had it, said the Earth Spirit. Man was little more than an empty, soulless *bhuta*. It was thus that Venus sent the mightiest being of the planet, Sanat Kumara, the Fire Lord, who descended upon Earth escorted by four great lords and a hundred attendants."

An author risks ridicule by employing a quote from Madame Blavatsky's *Book of Dzyan,* one of the mainstays of Theosophy, and allegedly one of mankind's "forbidden books." It is nevertheless an acceptable risk when dealing with the widespread notion that at some point in human prehistory (or "primohistory," as author Robert Char-roux termed it), entities from other worlds, whether spiritual or physical, descended upon the earth on a civilizing mission.

The Venusian lord Sanat Kumara and his retinue allegedly instructed primitive man in the skills of agriculture and beekeeping, much in the same way that Semjase's crew of Watchers went about the business of teaching the rudiments of civilization to the ever-attractive "daughters of men."

The Mesoamerican traditions of Ce-Acatl-Topiltzin-Quetzalcoatl, "Our Noble Prince, Feathered Serpent," whose link to the planet Venus is paramount throughout Aztec legend, represents another surprising corollary to the tutelary presence of the Biblical Watchers. Two versions of the Quetzalcoatl legend have survived to our times. The most familiar deals with the fall of the god-king who was deceived into having sexual intercourse with his sister (shades of Arthurian legend). In repentance, he built his own funeral pyre and apotheotically returned to the planet Venus. Using his "magic mirror" of pure obsidian, Tezcatlipoca showed Quetzalcoatl his reflection—that of a wizened old man with a skull-like face. Recoiling in horror, the god hid himself until his enemy lured him out again, intoxicating him with wine and leading him to his downfall.

The second version involves the timeless, titanic struggle between Tezcatlipoca (embodiment of the physical world) and Quetzalcoatl (representing the mind and spirit). Quetzalcoatl is a truly protean figure—a teacher, master of esoteric lore, a demiurge in a world gripped by awesome forces, giver of laws and civilization.

It is little wonder that so many Mexican rulers and high-priests assumed the cultural god's name, causing much confusion to archaeologists and historians of later centuries. There was even an order of priests named Quetzalcoatl, whose semi-monastic rule (predating Christian monasteries) urged them to emulate the kindness and holiness of the Feathered Serpent in every way.

All ancient records agree that Quetzalcoatl made the discovery that maize was suitable nourishment for his human subjects. This fact is a troubling one for modern scholars, since the cultivation of maize goes back some 9,000 to 10,000 years. Admitting the existence of a great civilizing force such as this so far into the past upsets the historical tables to no end, so this information is safely relegated into the realm of myth.

"Quetzalcoatl the Man"—to differentiate him from the deity—has been identified in recent times with an Irish monk, a Viking warrior, the Apostle Thomas, a Grand Master of the Knights Templar, and myriad other identities. But all evidence points toward an initial man or superman of that name existing nearly 10,000 years ago, at the very dawn of the Neolithic Age. His existence has been entwined with the mystery of timeless pyramids of Teotihuacan. This connection, coupled with the sheer antiquity of the site, have led some authors to make the fantastic claim that the "feathered serpent" emblem found at the Temple of Quetzalcoatl in Teotihuacan represents no modern reptile, but the head of a dinosaur millions of years old.

Benign, Malevolent, or Both?

ALTHOUGH "scientific" ufology cringes at the mention of any angelic/demonic involvement, the recent spate of abductions engulfing the world provides cases that could be seen within such a context. Abduction researcher Barbara Bartholic has singled out a case in which a youth faced what at first appeared to be a "Nordic" type of male alien who reverted into a reptilian form, assaulting the unsuspecting young man and leaving furrows across his back.

While this sobering incident is presented in the light of the shape-shifting ability of a particular alien race, it is strongly reminiscent of texts of a religious nature which state that demons can sometimes appear as "angels of light," which is what the tall, blond alien visitors have been associated with.

The dichotomy over whether the Watchers are benign or evil has been approached with the same caution reserved for the "good angel/bad angel" case. As in the fragment from the *Testament of Am-ram,* we can see the existence of two very different kinds of Watcher. Some yogis, for instance, believe that the Dark Angels have been confined to certain dimensions. Renaissance authors wrote of the nine-day-long fall of the vanquished angels into Hell, based upon Greek legends of the casting of the Cyclops into Tartaros—so distant that an anvil would take nine days to hit bottom. Could there be a connection between the negative order of beings and the allegedly extraterrestrial visitors we are entertaining today?

In 1947, one Señor C.A.V. encountered strange amoeba-like beings in the desert outside Lima, Peru, who took him aboard their landed vehicle. The conversation between the stunned Señor C.A.V. and his nonhuman hosts turned to spiritual matters. They replied mockingly to his question about God, stating: "We are like Gods." Either the beings had a very high opinion of themselves, or they ranked among the fallen Watchers.

In the Kwa Sizabantu mission station in South Africa, a woman approached German theologian Kurt Koch to confess a strange encounter in the Namib Desert with a robot-crewed UFO. In the course of a telepathic conversation with the mechanical aliens, one of them declared: "God is not going to answer your prayers anyway. But we can fulfill your wishes?'

More stories abound with regard to the benevolent Watchers, both in antiquity and in the present. A truly bewildering case of Watcher intervention into human life is submitted by Spanish UFO researcher Salvador Freixedo in his book *Ellos: Los Duenos Invisibles de este Mundo*. When a brush fire broke out on the estate of Colombian journalist Ines de Montana, farmhands ran to and fro trying to create fire breaks in the middle of the night. Enormous tongues of flame lapped at the black skies while the journalist and her trusted housekeeper, Jovita Caicedo, looked on in sheer terror.

The old wooden farmhouse from which they beheld the breeze, was about to be incinerated when "a helicopter of light," as de Montana describes it, swooped in from the western sky. The coruscate light came closer, as low as the tops of the coconut palms, leaving a wake like a comet's tail in its path. It then began to emit a blast of intense cold, which had the effect of extinguishing the raging fire, dousing it as effectively as would have tons of water.

Montana's incredible story was devoted an entire page in the newspaper for which she worked. "What you have read is the truth, supported by the testimony of four people who felt the effects of a strange phenomenon, and by the fact that in over 30 years, no one has been able to say that there has been fantasy, fiction or deceit in the thousands of words I've written," she stated.

Frank Smythe, a mountain climber ascending one of the Himalayan peaks, allegedly observed a "pulsating tea kettle" which seemed to be monitoring his progress. Smythe noted that before seeing it, he'd had the sensation of someone benignly watching his efforts.

It has been suggested that what we are seeing is "police activity" of a sort, on the behalf of the positive Watchers, as they go about their appointed rounds, fending off the attacks of the renegade contingent. While some may find this hard to accept, some confirmation can be found in events which took place in Spain during a very heavy period of UFO activity in that country in the early 1980s.

The town of Isla Cristina, on Spain's southern coast, was plagued by UFOs, giant creatures thrashing across the tidal swamps, and a host of other hair-raising and disturbing phenomena. Maria Echague, a resident of the town, witnessed two tall, slender, white-haired figures who appeared to move in unison some 40 meters from where she stood. Amazed by the odd beauty and synchronicity of movement displayed by the beings, Ms. Echague found herself thinking *"Que sois?"* (What are you?) The beings turned in unison to show her the raised thumb, index and middle fingers of their right hands (a classic esoteric gesture, symbolizing the triumph of spirit over matter) and mentally replied: "We are teachers," before disappearing.

The Watchers continue to stage spectacles for the benefit of those whom they contact and the spellbound followers of these "modern prophets" as well. Augusta de Almeidda, a contactee from the Philippines, was advised by her "alien brothers" that an aerial display of their majesty would take place over an arena on June 12, 1992. Four hundred onlookers witnessed golden spherical and cigar-shaped vehicles of varied geometry over the stadium at 8:05 P.M. that evening.

Conclusion

TALK of supernatural Watchers—"Sons of God" who mated with human females at the dawn of time and were cast out from their lofty position by divine powers—tends to annoy the believer in extraterrestrial visitors and/or ancient astronauts. But it would be both unrealistic and unwise to discount the strong paranormal component that exists in the angel/UFO phenomenon. Some expressions of this phenomenon echo the persistent notion of a primeval struggle between good and evil factions that is at the root of many different mythologies—the clash between Ormuz and Ahriman in Zoroastrianism, that between Ouranos and the Cyclops in Greek myth, the struggle between BacaabQuich, and Tohil in the Mayan cosmology, and the struggle between Quetzalcoatl and Tezcatlipoca.

As Amram cautioned his children in his testament: "I leave you my books in testimony, that you might be warned by them…"

WHAT DO ANGELS LOOK LIKE?

Rosemary Ellen Guiley

(Dec. 2005)

One reason it is so difficult to determine what angels are is that accounts describe them so very differently. Fate consulting editor Rosemary Ellen Guiley, author of The Encyclopedia of Angels, offers an enthralling overview of the many differing ways they have manifested themselves to humans throughout the years.

HOW do we know what angels look like? In encounters with angels, some people see human-like forms with wings, while others see pillars and balls of light. Do angels shape-shift? Can they take on any form?

Our ideas of the appearances of angels have been expressed in art for about 1,800 years. Angels in art have undergone many changes during those years. Modern anger images bear little resemblance to the angels drawn at the start of Christianity.

That angels can be depicted at all was the subject of a heated controversy in early Christianity and was a major factor in the church splitting in two. The church fathers inherited a flourishing angel cult based on Jewish and pagan beliefs. Jews prohibited religious images in general, but pagans—the great masses to be converted—expected them, in keeping with their own traditions of portraying gods and goddesses.

The church fathers were deeply divided on the desirability of any images of the sacred. Opponents of sacred images argued that incorporeal spirits could never be accurately portrayed in art. Any renderings would be misleading, and might encourage idol worship as well. Supporters of sacred images countered that people need and respond to images as a way of connecting to their faith.

In 325 the Church Council of Nicaea made belief in angels a part of dogma, which permitted artists to freely draw and sculpt them. But within the church, an intense controversy raged for more than 600 years. The issue was especially volatile in the Eastern Orthodox, or Byzantine, Church, where opponents of images believed them to be idols that fostered superstition and hindered the conversion of the Jews and Muslims. In Constantinople, Emperor Leo III launched persecutions against icon worship. People were arrested and icons were destroyed.

In Rome, an enraged Pope Gregory III declared that anyone who broke or defiled holy images would be excommunicated. Leo III retaliated by sending a naval fleet to Rome to punish the pope, but it was wrecked by storms.

Leo and his successors continued their campaign against sacred images in the East. In 842, icon worship was at last restored and the opponents were excommunicated. The rift between East and West was too large, however, and 20 years later the two churches split.

Today, images of the divine, including angels, are now incorporated into both Eastern and Western churches. Artistic styles diverged considerably. Eastern icons have a distinctive style which attempts to portray the tension between reality and abstraction, physicality and incorporeity. The Western angel has become a model of human perfection with wings. Both represent different aspects of the angel. The Eastern angel is transcendent and mysterious; the Western angel is the idealized human.

Do Angels Have Wings?

THE IMAGE of angels as human-like beings with wings did not become fixed in art until the fourth century. The evolution of the angel wing has a long history.

Wings denote spirituality and divine purpose, speed, and the ability to mediate between physical and nonphysical realms. Winged spiritual beings are an ancient idea, but one that developed in the West more so than in the East. Eastern deities, saints, and spiritual beings move about without the benefit of wings, which are not necessary to navigate in the world of illusion. In art, they are shown descending from the sky or hovering in the air, held up by the weightlessness of their own divinity.

The Bible offers little in the way of descriptions of angels. Judaism prohibits sacred images, so no renderings were inherited by the Christians. In Genesis, Abraham is visited by angels who appear as humans. In Tobit, Raphael, in the guise of a man, is a traveling companion for Tobias. The strange creatures seen by Ezekiel in a vision have wings and animal heads. There are also human figures clothed in brilliant light. The New Testament doesn't do much better. Gabriel, in announcing the pending birth of Jesus to Mary, merely "comes in" and "departs." The angel who announces the birth of Jesus to the shepherds appears "suddenly" in the night.

Accordingly, early angel art portrays angels as ennobled, ethereal male humans without wings. The earliest known image dates to the early third century, an image in the Catacomb of Priscilla in Rome. It portrays the Annunciation, with Gabriel looking like a tunic-clad man standing on the earth.

The man-like angel evolved into the winged, hovering angel during the fourth century. By the end of the fourth century, Christian artists had turned to the winged deities of pagan religions for inspiration. They borrowed heavily from the Greek idea that divinity has shape, and it is humanlike, and from the Roman image of Victory. However, they refrained from frank nakedness and sexuality. Their angels were adult males but without pronounced sexual characteristics—androgynous in appearance—and were fully clothed, with a standard tunic and mantle. Their wings often were not pronounced in size or detail. By the end of the fifth century, the winged, hovering angel had become standard.

The androgynous, hovering winged angel dominated angel art through the sixth century, and made appearances in European art through the 12th century. By the 14th century, theological interest in angels peaked and began to decline. The Inquisition focused attention on fallen angels—the demons who tempted people into sin and witchcraft. Demons were given ugly, bat-like wings by artists. The Reformation of the 16th century further diminished the importance of the heavenly angel.

As the angel became less important in theology, the image of the angel became more glorious in art. Renaissance artists portrayed angels as beautiful male youths and women. The decline of the angel produced some of the greatest and most beautiful angel art: glorious beings with enormous, elegant wings and exquisite, flowing garments. Artists used eagles and swans for models of wings. They painted wings with rainbow hues. The rainbow is a symbol of the bridge to heaven, and underscores the angel's role as intermediary between heaven and earth.

Renaissance art left a lasting impact on popular conceptions of angels. The angel as idealized human continues to dominate angel art. Many modern angels are brought even further down to human level with country clothes and pigtails.

Angels in Modern Visionary Encounters

DESPITE what we think angels "should" look like, most modern accounts of encounters with angels do *not* involve beings with wings. Visual apparitions usually are of balls of white or white-gold light, or of columns or pillars of light that vaguely resemble or suggest human form. Sometimes such figures seem to be wearing flowing, glowing white drapery that suggests the shape of wings, but without clear definition.

41

ANGELS AND HEAVENLY VISITATIONS

One of the most common angel experiences is the "mysterious stranger," an unknown person who comes along suddenly and mysteriously to solve a problem or crisis, and then disappears without a trace. Such figures have a stronger relationship to the man-like figures in Genesis and. Tobit than to the swan-winged figures in art.

Angels can be regarded as the ultimate shape-shifters. They take whatever form suits the human needs and yearnings of the moment.

HOW I SPOKE WITH THE ANGELS

Gustav Gumpert
(April 1961)

Paranormal researcher Gustav Gumpert's account of how he used an Ouija board to make contact with angelic beings and the answers they gave to his questions belies the recent movie phenomenon, Ouija, *which portrays the Ouija board as a dangerous instrument which demonic forces can use as a gateway for entering our world. Gumpert's account is one of the pieces readers have requested* Fate *reprint most often. It has been reprinted three times in the magazine and at least twice in books compiled from* FATE's *pages.*

WHERE do Ouija board messages come from? From the unconscious minds of the operators? From beings dwelling in a world beyond? Or are they telepathic communications?

These were the questions that filled our minds as a friend and I hunched over the Ouija board one snowy night last winter.

We were determined to make a calm and objective experiment. Actually, we were about to get the shock of our lives; for we received a series of messages that reversed our opinion on the chances of communicating with a world beyond the senses.

As the pointer slid evenly, deliberately across the board, we saw spelled out before our astonished eyes a message that never could have come from either of our minds. It was in a language neither of us knew, one no man has ever spoken.

But let's begin at the beginning.

The first part of the message was in English: "This is Raphael." Then we received a brilliant lecture on occult philosophy that, when written down, filled one notebook page.

This much, we decided, could have bubbled up from our unconscious minds. We both had read a little in the literature of occultism. We knew that Raphael, along with Gabriel, Michael and Uriel, were the four archangels of the ancient Hebrew's angelic hierarchy. So we were dissatisfied; what we wanted was a test that would definitely rule out the chances of our unconsciously collaborating with the board.

We challenged the Ouija—or whatever was operating it—to give us proof beyond any question.

The next message seemed at first glance like a string of nonsense syllables: ECA RAFAEL OD VAOAN I OD IAODPIL TAI.

We first thought, quite naturally that this was pure gibberish. But a certain precision about the movements of the pointer aroused our suspicion. Instead of moving wildly, as one might expect, it moved with a decisiveness that suggested intelligent and conscious direction.

"Let's go on with it," I said. "We may be getting something after all."

The rest of the message came through slowly: MICALZO I IADON OD MICALZO T CMS QAAIAD. IADON EL IL OD CAOSGI NOQS IA.

It is only fair to say that between the two of us we read or speak eight languages—German, English, French, Dutch, Spanish, Italian, Latin and Greek. We also have a smattering of some of the Slavic tongues; and I had once taken a brief and not very useful course in Hindustani. Moreover, I always have been keenly interested in linguistics and cryptograms.

Both of us are rather widely read in the history of art and archeology. We had probably seen—and stored in the unconscious—fragments of the ancient languages that appear on archeological remains.

It seemed to us probable, then, that we were receiving a scrambled version from our unconscious minds of all these languages and recollections. We certainly didn't expect the language to mean anything—and we never dreamed that anyone else might have heard of it. We were wrong on both counts.

There was one clue to the mystery. Flickering in the recesses of my memory was a recollection that somewhere I had read about a strange language that had been discovered in England centuries ago by two mystics. It stuck in my mind that this language was supposed to have been spoken by an angel.

For those who may feel skeptical at this point, let me say that I never had seen any samples of this hidden language. Somewhere in my reading I had seen a reference made to Dr. John Dee, court astrologer to Queen Elizabeth. The article said that Dee, in collaboration with a man named Edward Kelley, had received and recorded messages in a language he learned from an angel.

On the basis of pure hunch, then, we decided to look up the original writings received in this peculiar language. We found that we were looking for a book by Meric Casaubon entitled "A True & Faithful Relation of what passed for many years Between Dr. John Dee (A Mathematician of Great Fame in Q. Eliz. and King James their Reignes) and Some Spirits." The volume was published in 1659. These strange communications from beyond also may be found in Sloane Manuscripts 31893191 in the British Museum.

Quickly scanning the 13 pages of recorded messages, my eye fell on the first word we had received through the Ouija board: ECA. It meant "therefore."

But before giving you the translation of our messages, let me say a word about Dee and Kelley . . . .

John Dee was born in London, of wealthy parents, in 1527. He first studied at Cambridge University and later at universities in France, Germany and Holland. After the death of Queen (Bloody) Mary, he became court astrologer to Queen Elizabeth. He died in 1608.

Edward Kelley was a medium, who was well known in London during the same period. He foretold, four years in advance, the execution of Queen Mary and the coming of the Spanish Armada, and he claimed to get his information from spirits. Dee decided to hire Kelley as a "scryer" or crystal gazer, at a salary of 50 pounds a year.

After gazing in his crystal for a while, Kelley was told to construct four large charts (49 inches square) and to fill the columns with certain letters. The two men did this. Then the angel, who said he was Gabriel, would point to a letter on similar charts which Kelley saw in the crystal. Kelley would call out the information, Dee wrote it down.

By this laborious method, the two men were given 19 "Angelic Calls," which were supposed to be powerful evocations for calling up spirits. So far as anyone knows the messages never were used for that purpose until the 1880's, when they were adopted by the Order of the Golden Dawn, a group of English mystics which for a time included the poet W. B. Yeats among its members. The rituals of this group, published in America in 1940 by a member of the Order, Israel Regardie, show that the Angelic Calls were used for magical purposes.

But to return to our story. At this point we had 13 pages of "Angelic," with its translation—but no dictionary of the language. How were we to find out what the words in our message meant?

We decided to prepare a dictionary, rather than look through the whole 13 pages for each word. It took three days to compile the dictionary. When completed, it consisted of 800 entries. In the course of the work we discovered that the language had genuine syntax and logical structure. The verbs were conjugated and the nouns declined.

Take for example the word "say."

"I say" is GOHUS; "he says" is GOHO; "we say" is GOHIA; "saying" is GOHOL; "said" is GOHON; and "it is said" is GOHULIM.

We also found that some of the words went back to the most ancient recorded speech. To give just one example: Latin scholars long have puzzled about the words Flamen Dialis, used to describe the Roman high priest of Jupiter. Flamen means "priest," but Dial is not a true Latin word. Strangely enough, though, Dial is a word in Angelic. It is one of the names of God. So that Flamen Dialis means "Priest of God."

Here is the translation of the first message we received: "Therefore Raphael exists, and Truth exists, and the Everlasting God dwells amongst you. Mighty is the Lord in His creations. He is the world, in which He operates, and it is His servant."

From that day on the messages continued, mostly in English but with occasional phrases in Angelic. To date, we have received enough material to fill 40 pages of typescript, outlining an amazing system of occult philosophy.

Here are some of the questions we asked and the answers we received. Remember that these were spelled out, a letter at a time, on the Ouija board:

March 5, 1960:

Q: Is there any point in studying the Angelic language?

A: Yes. The sounds have great power, like music, and stir the unconscious into motion. This was a great revelation, and can profit you much.

April 18, 1960:

Q: What is reality?

A: The world as you see and know it is not the true world. The world of your senses is one of many possible worlds. You will never understand this until you have experienced the greater view of the universe, which is what men mean when they speak of enlightenment. This is the meaning of the Japanese Zen Satori, the meaning of the Buddha when he spoke of Nirvana, and of Jesus when he spoke of Heaven.

April 19, 1960:

Q: What is Heaven?

A: A state of mind, open to all men, which comes through careful following of the path. It is a new experience of the universe, which shows the many worlds within the one world and the one world within the many.

Q: What is required for faith healing?

A: To be a healer, one must first learn to release the unconscious, as all power of the earthly type flows from this source. Secondly, you must learn to focus this unconscious power on one problem at a time. The unconscious operates when you are asleep. Therefore, before going to sleep, concentrate on one subject. Limit your concentration to one phrase or sentence of not more than ten words. Repeat this over and over. Your unconscious will do the rest; you will achieve the objective. April 25, 1960:

Q: Does sex stand in the way of enlightenment?

A: The physical and spiritual are of one substance. By making a distinction, you create a problem where none exists. Salvation is not against life. It is life, and life is physical as well as spiritual: each has its own place in the unity of the whole. May 2, 1960:

Q: What is time?

A: There is no time as you know it. Everything in the universe is an experience occurring simultaneously. You perceive this in parts. That is what you mean by time.

May 7, 1960:

Q: Is there life after death?

A: Time has no beginning or ending, nor do you. It is as though you walked through a series of rooms. Each room is there and continues to exist after you depart from it. Before you enter, it is the future; and after you leave, it is the past. But the room is always there—it is you who change. You will always continue, for you are a great circle that begins nowhere and ends nowhere.

May 9, 1960:

Q: What is mind?

A: The function of the mind is not clearly understood by science. The mind is not the brain. On the contrary, the brain is an instrument that is used by the mind to achieve its purpose. The mind in turn is part of a total system, and this system cannot be fully comprehended unless it is experienced. The brain is an electronic system; the mind is a multi-dimensional system, greater than the brain in more than size. It is like putting the ocean in a bottle to try to understand the mind with the brain. Therefore, resign yourself to the fact that you will never understand the mind: you can only experience it. For if you try to understand the greater with the lesser, what can you learn?

In addition to these messages, Raphael has given many examples of independent knowledge of facts, events and situations we could not have known. Most of these are personal, however, and cannot be reported here.

This remarkable experience raises a number of questions. How can we explain, by any rational method, the message in Angelic—before either of us, the operators, had seen the language? Most remarkable of all, I think, this experience has caused two hard-headed sceptics to question their own explanations of the universe.

For, if we can talk with angels, what kind of world do we really live in?

PART II
ANGELIC ENCOUNTERS OF THE RICH AND/OR FAMOUS

*F*OR SOME REASON *people seem more likely to believe new or difficult ideas if they come from the mouth of someone who is famous. In this section, we offer true stories of angelic encounters recounted by stars, musicians, authors, politicians and other celebrities.*

ROY ORBISON AND THE THREE ANGELS

Leon Thompson

(Dec. 2000)

Country and western great, Roy Orbison, whose complex melodies and operatic singing style led to his being called "the Caruso of rock," believed in angels. In this very personal reminiscence WWII vet Leon Thompson, a friend of Orbison's, describes an angelic messenger the late singing great sent on a mission no one but he and Orbison could have known about.

A S WE WATCHED TV on New Year's Eve, the old year slipped away with fireworks blasting through the air, bells ringing, and all kinds of noise. When the doorbell rang at first, I did not want to stop watching TV to go answer it. But when it rang a second time, I walked to the door and opened it. There stood the most beautiful woman I have ever seen in all my years. She was so much like the statue of Helen of Troy that I didn't notice what she had in her hands when she began speaking with me.

Her hair was like gold and her looks were outstanding. Her perfume was strong like a rose. I was at a loss for words, but slowly she began to tell me that she had an object that belonged in the Roy Orbison Room Lounge at the Wink, Texas, Airport.

A Celestial Meeting

I T SHOULD HAVE been dark outside, but for some reason the entire front yard took on a soft, yellow glow and a warmth that I have never felt in my life. As I stood looking, she presented me with a cherub-like figure. It was about 12 inches tall and made of something like papier-mâché.

The mystery woman told me that she was pleased that the other two small angels someone had left at the house before had gone to the right people. These two little angels were both crying and held a tear in their hands. One went to Mayor E. Jones of Wink, Texas, where it now sits on her desk for everyone to see, and the other angel went to Richard West, a close friend of Roy Orbison. (The mayor's angel was sent to encourage her to promote Roy Orbison; Richard West's angel was sent because his only sister was due to pass on from this world.)

How she knew all this I had no way of knowing. But as the fireworks exploded in the New Year's night, she challenged me to remember the time that Roy Orbison and I went searching for the Miracle Site in Wink—and were met by three angels.

Well did I recall the incident in 1949 when we saw three fog-like forms. Roy said they were real angels, but I did not see any such thing. Roy told me they said the reason I could not see them was because I did not believe in them.

I remember telling Roy that if he ever went to the "other side," he should tell the angels that I do believe. So here was this beautiful woman trying to explain things to me. However, her "third angel" was so vastly different from the other two she spoke about that I questioned it.

I was fascinated by her lovely voice, and her beauty seemed out of this world. When I looked at her feet, I saw beautiful white and gold slip-on shoes. "Yes, we do wear shoes when we wish to do so!" she told me.

I turned to call my friend to the door, but he was slow in answering. As I turned again to speak with the woman, she was gone, and the warm glow that had filled the front yard slowly dimmed until it was dark again. When my friend came to the door, he refused to believe that the woman had been there. He could not understand, however, where I had acquired the unique little cherub I was now holding.

Slowly, the New Year's fireworks ceased and it was so quiet that my ears rang without sound. We both looked at the cherub the woman had given me. It was beautiful beyond words and so light to the touch.

Message From a Friend

FOR THE NEXT WEEK I could not get the strange woman out of my mind. How quickly she had vanished! We searched the yard—though there was no place to hide, we found no trace of her.

I began to have odd dreams about the first two angels that were smaller and so different. Eventually, we wrapped up the little cherub and shipped it to Charlie Cooper, who operated the Roy Orbison Room Lounge at the Wink, Texas, Airport.

Reflecting on my conversation with the woman, something I had not realized before began to sink into my dull mind: Roy had mentioned that the angels he had seen were without shoes. As if in response, the woman had said that "we do wear shoes when we wish to do so!"

Other things crept into my mind, too, and it struck me like a bolt of lightning—I had seen and had talked with the "third angel" that Roy Orbison and I had met at the Miracle Site in 1949.

Here was the answer to my question about real angels. Here was the fulfillment of my request to send me a real angel, and it had happened so quickly and unexpectedly that it took a while for the truth to soak into my dull head. Here was the Third Angel to answer all the questions that I had asked back in 1949.

Faraway Music

TODAY, the little cherub angel can be seen in the Roy Orbison Room Lounge at the Wink Airport. It hangs among the other items that once belonged to Roy when he lived in Wink. Some say the little angel has a healing power if you know how to use it. Others mention that the little angel is attractive and a unique addition to the Roy Orbison Room where it now hangs. Some have said that they pray for others when they visit the lounge, but no one has come up with real proof of a miracle so far. In silence the little angel seems to be playing a musical instrument; at times, a few people have said they have heard a faraway musical chord when they were alone with it for a time.

The little angel is proof that the late Roy Orbison was able to send an angel to speak with me as requested, which is something beyond my comprehension.

If you are ever in Wink, Texas, take time to visit the Roy Orbison Room Lounge and see if the little angel still plays a silent tune for those who wish to believe—and for those who need to believe—in angels.

I for one no longer doubt angels—they do exist, somehow, somewhere.

WILLIAM BLAKE, THE MAN WHO SAW (AND TALKED WITH) ANGELS

Robert T. Taylor

(Jan. 1954)

One world famous poet and artist, William Blake, saw angels and heavenly visitors from a very early age. These encounters formed the basis of both his writings and paintings. Though Blake was unable to sell his work during his life time, today the original work he produced sells for prices he could never have imagined.

STRANGE THINGS were visible to William Blake even when he was only four years old. One day he ran screaming in childish terror from a window, because he saw God's face there. A few years later his mother whipped him for insisting that he had seen the prophet Ezekiel sitting in the fields near his home. When he was eight and on a ramble through Peckham Rye, he was startled by the sight of a group of angels sitting in a tree. Such visions appeared to him throughout his entire life. They were not sudden manifestations produced by illness, or insanity. He enjoyed robust health and his mind remained keen and clear up to the very moment of his death.

Except possibly for his Irish blood, which made him a member of a romantic race with a faith in supernatural forces, there was nothing in Blake's background to account for his visions. He was born on November 28, 1757; the third child of James and Catherine Blake. His father was a London hosier, not too prosperous, with a small shop at 28 Broad Street, Golden Square.

Blake's birth took place in the year to which the prophet Emanuel Swedenborg ascribed magical properties—the year 1757 that marked the beginning of a new age in which the kingdom of God appeared among men. It was an age that produced new intellectual and spiritual restlessness. In France and in America it culminated in revolutions. In England, it was marked by a departure from classical traditions and the Reign of Reason, to a revival of liberal ideas and the dawn of the Romantic Movement.

It was an age in which an underlying mysticism and superstition came to the surface. It drew men to the mysteries of freemasonry and intensified an almost universal belief in sorcery and astrology. It saw the growth of the Cabalist Lodges of Martinez-Pasqualis, as well as the sensations created by the theories of Mesmer and the miracles of Cagliostro. It introduced the mystic doctrines of Swedenborg and Boehme.

Blake reflected this turbulent age in his vigor, beliefs and talents. Like most geniuses, he was precocious. He painted before he was ten and wrote voluminously when he was 12. His first published poems, the *Poetical Sketches,* were written before he was 18 and yet seemed mature.

He received little formal education. His peculiarities made his parents reluctant to send him to school and he was taught at home.

Under ordinary circumstances, he was well enough equipped for life, particularly for his father's shop. But for a man of letters the Authorized Version of the Bible and the poetry of Milton, the ideas of Swedenborg and of his father, a religious radical who delighted in theological discussions with his friends, provided scant background. Had he received proper guidance he might have risen to even greater literary heights than he did. As it was, the random seeding of his fertile mind produced the chaotic harvest of his later works.

The only real training Blake received was in art. His mother was sympathetic toward his love of drawing and when it became obvious that he was not temperamentally fitted for work in his father's shop he was sent to Henry Pars' drawing school in the Strand, where he remained from the time he was ten till he was 14.

When Blake left Pars' school it was clear that he should be placed under some well-known painter. But a large premium was required and Blake was unwilling to be favored at the expense of the other children in his family. He suggested engraving as a suitable substitute and was taken to Ryland, then engraver to the king.

As a result of his uncanny insight, Blake took an instant dislike to Ryland. He remarked to his father, "I do not like the man's face; it looks as if he will live to be hanged." Twelve years later Ryland actually was hanged. He had fallen into debt and committed a forgery on the East India Company.

Blake was next taken to the studio of James Basire to whom, for a premium of 50 guineas, he was apprenticed to learn the art of engraving. Basire was a kindly man and a good teacher and Blake soon learned to copy to the other's satisfaction. Basire sent Blake to draw the Gothic monuments in Westminster Abbey and other churches, trusting him not to abuse the privilege. Blake spent several years at this task, copying throughout the summer and engraving his drawings during the winter.

Though he spent long hours in the gloomy corners of cathedrals, Blake was never lonesome. His visions kept him company. The statues he drew came to life for him. While working in Westminster Abbey he was visited by Christ and the apostles.

In 1778 Blake's apprenticeship to Basire ended and. he joined the antique class of the Royal Academy. Shortly after this he began to earn his living as an engraver. When Blake was 25 he met Catherine Boucher, the daughter of a market-gardener with whom he boarded during a vacation at Battersea. At the first sight and with a shock that forced her to leave the room, Catherine recognized him as her future husband.

Catherine was a sympathetic listener and Blake confided to her that an unhappy love affair had driven him from London. Deeply affected by his story she said that she was sorry for him.

"Do you pity me?" Blake asked in his impulsive way. "Then I love you for that."

This was the beginning of their relationship and engagement; though Blake and Catherine were separated for one year, until he had money enough to provide a home for her. They were married on August 18, 1782.

Blake was fortunate in his choice of a wife. Catherine was uneducated but she proved a perfect companion for a man of his unusual talents. Their marriage was for the most part a happy one, though Catherine once was heard to complain: "I have very little of Mr. Blake's company. He is always in Paradise."

She accompanied Blake on long walks that would have tired most women. She arose in the middle of the night to keep him company when he was driven to work by his fierce inspirations. She managed their slim finances so cleverly that Blake hardly was aware of the many times they existed on the verge of actual hardship. For his sake and with his help, she learned to read and write and even to draw and color in order to help him. She believed completely in Blake's visions and regarded him as above ordinary men.

This was not true of the other persons who came into contact with Blake. Most people found his ideas strange and disturbing and it was this in his poetry and Art that kept him from achieving popular recognition and success.

He might have found wealthy patrons had he been willing to sacrifice pride and independence. But on his few excursions into fashionable society he proved too honest and direct to be ingratiating. He would not accept criticism, was firm in his opinion and dogmatic in his assertions. He knew he possessed unusual abilities and he regarded all, no matter how famous and respected, who differed with him as fools. He never stood in awe of public opinion. His visions gave him absolute confidence in himself.

Blake was below average in height but strong and well-built. His light-colored hair was touched with gold and stood up from his high forehead in a way that reminded his friends of a lion's mane. His eyes were striking, unusually large and of piercing brilliance. He possessed great vitality and could work for many hours without fatigue.

His expression has been described as serene and kind. It accurately mirrored his inner self, for he preached charity and tolerance and also practiced it. On numerous occasions he gave generously of his meager funds to help others out of difficulty.

It was these qualities in his character, as much as his genius, that endeared him to his few close friends and made them willing to overlook his eccentricities. Men like Flaxman, Fuseli, Tatham and Butts remained loyal to him all his life but were unable to be of much actual help, simply because Blake was not an easy man to help.

In 1784 Blake went into business selling prints in Broad Street, next door to his brother James who had taken over the hosier's shop after the death of their father. An acquaintance of his apprentice days named Parket went into partnership with Blake, but this was soon dissolved.

At this time Blake's younger brother, Robert, came to live with him and to serve as an apprentice. Robert was Blake's favorite brother and when he fell sick after three years, Blake nursed Robert devotedly, staying at his side night and day during the two weeks before he died. As Robert breathed his last Blake saw his soul rising into Heaven "clapping its, hands for joy." Blake regarded death as nothing more final than going into another room. He was confident that he would continue to see Robert—and he did.

Robert appeared to Blake in a dream and revealed an entirely original process for printing books. His earliest poems, the *Poetical Sketches,* had been printed with the help of his friend Flaxman and Mr. and Mrs. Matthew, a sophisticated couple who liked to surround themselves with artistic and literary celebrities. But Blake was unable to find a publisher for his subsequent works and was too poor to pay to have them printed. Robert's revelation thus pointed the way out of a literary blind alley.

The new process involved the engraving of words and designs on small copper plates. These were first outlined with an acid-resistant, stopping-out varnish. Then the white parts of the plate were eaten out with acid, so that the outlined parts stood in relief. From these plates pages were printed in different colors and the surrounding designs afterward tinted by hand, so that words and pictures blended in a harmonious, artistic effect. That this method required engraving every word in reverse gives an idea of the superhuman patience involved.

In this unusual and exacting fashion Blake printed and illuminated all of his later books—the *Songs of Innocence* and the *Songs of Experience,* the prophetic books, *Urizen, Los,* and the *Marriage of Heaven and Hell.* These editions are as unique as the man who created them and today are extremely rare and valuable. Yet at the time they were published they found few buyers, even at the price of a few guineas a copy.

Blake's printing and illustrating of his own books were but a few of his many accomplishments. He also wrote beautiful poetry and drew strikingly original designs and on occasion, particularly during his visits to the home of the Matthews, showed that he possessed great talent as a composer. Until he was repelled by the sham of their snobbish world, Blake enlivened the Matthews' parties by setting his poems to music and singing them. These songs are said to have been remarkably beautiful.

All this from a single man and that man largely inexperienced and untrained! His melodies, for instance, do not survive today because he lacked the technical knowledge of musical notation.

Blake's political beliefs were as radical as his creative works. He was deeply stirred by the French Revolution and until the Terror of September, 1792, openly wore the red cap of liberty. For a while he attended the meetings of a small group of revolutionaries at the home of a bookseller named Johnson. Among the persons he met here was Thomas Paine, author of the *Rights of Man.*

Blake's psychic perceptions saved Paine from arrest, and possibly from hanging . After one of Paine's inflammatory speeches Blake warned him that he was in danger and not to return home. That same night soldiers went to Paine's house to arrest him but he had taken Blake's advice and fled to France.

One of the high points of Blake's life came in 1800 when he went to live at Felpham in Sussex, to be near William Hayley, while engraving the illustrations for Hayley's *Life of Cowper.* Hayley was wealthy and liked to pose as a literary figure, though he lacked imagination and was a bad poet. He was partly motivated by self-interest in acting as Blake's patron. He enjoyed helping others only as long as they were of service.

At first Blake was very happy at Felpham. In a letter to Flaxman he wrote:

"Felpham is a sweet place for study; because it is more spiritual than London. Heaven opens here on all sides her golden gates; her windows are not obstructed by vapors; voices of celestial inhabitants are most distinctly heard, and their forms more distinctly seen; and my cottage is also a shadow of their houses. . ."

During his stay at Felpham his glimpses of other world sights were most numerous: One day he witnessed a poignant event: "I was walking alone in my garden; there was great stillness among the branches and flowers, and more than common sweetness in the air; I heard a low and pleasant sound, and I knew not whence it came. At last I saw the broad leaf of a flower mote, and, underneath, I saw a procession of creatures of the size and color of green and grey grasshoppers, bearing a body laid out on a rose leaf, which they buried with songs, and then disappeared. It was a fairy funeral."

At Felpham Blake also saw "majestic shadows, grey but luminous, and superior to the common height of men." These were the spiritual forms of great men of old, of Moses and the prophets, Homer, Dante and Milton. They spoke to him in words he alone could hear, describing the life of their mysterious realms and revealing the secrets of ages yet to come. These things, cloaked in symbolism, were included in his poems, many of which he claimed were dictated to him by his invisible mentors. He stood in awe of these poems and never attempted to revise them, since he felt they were not his.

But at the very moments when Blake's visions were clearest and his inspirations most urgent, he found Hayley taking up his time with uninteresting tasks. Some tasks, like a commission to paint a fire screen for a lady, Blake flatly refused to do. Hayley grew impatient and soon openly voiced his disapproval of the work Blake was doing. For these reasons, although he maintained friendly relations with Hayley for some time afterward, Blake presently parted company with the man.

Blake returned to London in 1804 and entered a period during which he was more creative and productive than ever before. These years of his life are marked by such achievements as the two long poems *Jerusalem* and *Milton*, the famous *Descriptive Catalogue*, Blake's only prose work, and numerous superb paintings and engravings, especially those for the *Canterbury Pilgrims*, Blair's *Grave*, Dante's *Divine Comedy*, and *The Book of Job*. The paintings and engravings show more clearly than his poems how intensely absorbed Blake was in his supernatural existence.

Yet Blake was ignored by the public. An exhibition of his paintings in 1809 was a complete failure. Critics derided him, calling him a lunatic and saying that his paintings were filled with deformity and nonsense.

Blake found consolation in his visions. They opened for him vistas and glories that made him forget the world and its indifference. He withdrew into his invisible realms further than before. He had never concerned himself with public acclaim, for his works were neither about living men nor for them. He expressed his views in a letter to Flaxman:

"1 am more famed in Heaven for my works than I could well conceive. In my brain are studies and chambers filled with books and pictures, which I wrote and painted in ages of eternity before my mortal life, and those works are the delight and study of the arch-angels. Why, then, should I be anxious about the fame and riches of mortality?"

Now the spirits of great men of the past were visible and audible to him, and they also came to him at his call. He amazed his friends by summoning and drawing any dead person they named. In company with John Varley, the painter and astrologer he met in 1818, he often spent the entire night in this task. Varley would suggest subjects to Blake, unendingly fascinated by the prompt cry of "There he is!" with which Blake hailed the arrival of the spirit named.

Occasionally these awesome demonstrations were given a touch of mundane humor. Once while painting William Wallace, a Thirteenth Century Scot, Blake suddenly stopped and apologetically announced that he could not go on with the portrait because Edward I of England stood in front of Wallace. Not until Blake drew the face of the vain Edward could he finish his drawing of the Scot.

Sometimes Blake's ghostly visitors would not remain still. "He frowns," Blake would say. "He is displeased with my portrait of him." Or, "I can't go on—he is gone."

One night Blake became very excited and told Varley that he had seen the ghost of a flea—an unusual experience even for Blake. Varley urged him to paint the vision and the result was a naked monstrosity in human form, colored in shining green and gold, with demonic features and burning eyes fixed greedily on a cup of blood grasped between sharp claws. It was not a true ghost, Blake made this clear, but, rather a spiritualization of the flea which had been revealed to him. This painting, together with the spirit portraits, survives to this day.

Another important new friend Blake made in 1818 was the landscape painter John Linnell. Along with Varley and Butts, Linnell became a steady purchaser of Blake's work. These men were among the few who paid Blake fair prices and due to their sympathetic awareness of his genius, he did not exist in poverty. Their companionship also was important to him. Linnell in particular opened his home to Blake and introduced him to other patrons.

About this time a group of admiring young artists gathered around Blake to become his devoted disciples. Convinced of his talent and sanity, they did not criticize his mystical life. Blake thus was able to spend his last years in a secure and convivial atmosphere.

ANGELS AND HEAVENLY VISITATIONS

In 1827 Blake, now a gentle old man of 70, began to decline. There was no real illness, only a gradual sinking. On the day of his death, August 12, his visions became even more splendid and clear. His face grew radiant with happiness and he began to sing hymns. He died so peacefully that his wife, who sat at his bedside, was unable to tell the moment when he ceased breathing.

He now had entered completely that invisible world where he spent so much of his life and which he knew so much better than our own. He entered not as a stranger but as one who at long last had come home.

CLARK GABLE AND THE ANGEL'S ADVICE

Dana Howard

(Aug. 1961)

Dana Howard, a celebrated journalist in his day, was a believer in the mystical and the paranormal. That may be why motion picture superstar Clark Gable chose to share one of the most secret aspects of his early life with Howard, as recounted in the following anecdote.

CLARK GABLE'S sudden death has revived in my memory the days when his name first began to appear in the theaters of the world. An article of mine, titled "Substitute Fatherhood," had just been published in *Psychology Magazine* when I first met Mr. Gable.

I had covered the court trial where Mr. Gable was accused of fathering an illegitimate child; the accuser was a love-crazed English woman suffering from a paranoid quirk. Gable's good sportsmanship ruled his actions then, just as it continued to rule through the ensuing years. And, although this poor woman was dragging his name through the mire, he took it with good grace and warm tolerance. When the verdict against her claim was reached, Gable quietly paid her expenses back to England. I do not know whether this is generally known, but it was after the publication of my magazine article that Mr. Gable sent for Art Solomon, my editor, and I went along to talk about the problem.

At that time I was on the staff of the Ullman Publications, in their Hollywood office, and had gone to New York to cover the trial. As he sat in his dressing room at MGM studio, Mr. Gable unfolded the story that has remained etched in my consciousness, although nearly 30 years have passed since then. He called it "three-day amnesia." However, considered in the light of occult knowledge, I believe it was an experience in the supernormal. At any rate, it laid the cornerstone for his career as an all-time great in motion picture history.

As a review of his life will reveal, Clark Gable was not born to riches and greatness. In his youth he worked very hard for everything he obtained from life. He was a roustabout in the oil fields. He chivied logs in the great northwest. Anything and everything that paid a living wage, he pursued.

Meanwhile, he yearned to become an actor.

His first real opportunity in the theatre was the leading role in an intense drama called *Blind Windows*. This was around 1932 in New York. For weeks he had put every ounce of his emotional intensity into rehearsals. His body was weary with fatigue. His mind was filled with fog-banked hopes. Then one Friday night, tired and spent, he started a long walk.

"It seemed to me I was walking out on the pier," he told us. "I hadn't gone far when I came face to face with a dirty, ragged, disheveled tramp. 'Where yo' goin' bo?' he asked. I replied, 'I'm going for a swim.'"

Gable stated the tramp looked him over before answering. Then with a smirk on his face he said: "But you ain't goin' to be needin' them duds where you're goin'. Git 'em off." Gable said he didn't attempt to argue. It was apparent the man needed a new suit of clothes, so the exchange of raiment was made. Then, as an afterthought, the tramp asked for his money. Without a moment's hesitancy Gable told him that every dime he had in the world was in the pocket of his pants—$30 in all. He bid the tramp good-bye and moved on down the pier.

A little farther along he met another man—a kindly, elderly gentleman. His clothes had seen better days, but they were of fine material, and spotlessly clean.

"His was the kindest, most beautiful, male face I had ever seen," Gable said. "He was like someone from another world."

"Where are you going, young man?" he asked in a clear resonant voice. "I'm going for a swim," Gable replied.

They chatted for a few moments; then the older man asked, "Why not come home with me?" Somehow it seemed like a good suggestion, and there was something about the man Gable couldn't resist. He went along home with him.

"To this day I do not know where that home was," he told me. "But it was the cleanest, homiest place I had ever seen. It was simply furnished but there was a restfulness and a sense of security there."

The man had a daughter and, as Clark Gable described her, she was beautiful beyond words, with beauty of soul and beauty of body. She was affectionate in her greeting and was soon preparing coffee and sandwiches for him. She was like a lithe angel moving about the apartment. She held him in spellbound fascination, he said.

"I had met plenty of feminine pulchritude," he said. "But no woman affected me as she did. There was nothing sensual about it. I felt I was in the presence of an angel. Then before retiring she kissed me goodnight. It

62

was not a kiss of the flesh. It was a kiss of the spirit."

Then the old man sat him down at a table and looking him straight in the eye he began to draw him a word picture of the years to come. He told Clark Gable of his own life. "I was once very famous," he said. "I was very wealthy. I was married to a woman I loved very dearly." And he also told him that possessions are only loaned to one for the duration; they must eventually be surrendered.

"And so I gave fame away," the old man said. "And then I gave wealth away. Finally, I gave personalized love away." He spoke of humility and sacrifice. Of the fickle public that one day cheers, the next day sneers. He told of the pitfalls of too much money. He warned against the seductiveness of women. He instructed him in the higher values of life. In short he gave him the do's and the don'ts for the pattern of his coming success. There in that room which Mr. Gable could not identify, his future was mapped out.

Monday morning came and Mr. Gable returned to normal consciousness. But there now were three days missing from his life. He went to rehearsal. Lunch time came. He started his walk down Broadway to his usual eating place. Suddenly, about 50 yards ahead of him he saw her—the old man's daughter. He started toward her, jostling the crowd. He tried to call to her but in his breathless hurry the words did not carry. Finally he caught up with her. But she paid no attention to him. He reached out to touch her shoulder and his hand went through thin air. The girl was not there!

The most outstanding quotation I remember from what Clark Gable said is: "There in that place where there was neither money nor the things we strive for, I felt a sense of peace and happiness approaching the supernatural. That strange interlude influenced me beyond anything I have ever experienced. In that three days I lost out of my life I found myself."

Following this trans-dimensional experience Clark Gable enjoyed more than 30 years of epoch-making success.

There are many occult factors involved. First came the intensity of his zeal; this role in *Blind Windows* was the part he had hoped for. He turned on his personal dynamo full speed. Suddenly something exploded. The break-through came and suddenly his consciousness was released into the Great Unknown. It reached another dimension. Without losing his own identity, in that moment, Clark Gable became a universal citizen.

Let's examine the symbolism of the dream. Clark Gable went out on the pier: he was experiencing an extension of consciousness. He was going for a swim: a form of ablution, a preparation for a new life. He exchanged his one good suit of clothes for the tramp's rags: a lesson in humility and sacrifice. Thus he earned the privilege of penetrating the next dimension where he met a soul who drafted the years ahead and, at the same time, made him know that fame is transient; that money, too, is on loan from the Universal Bank. He told him also that personal love is the essence of God's love; that one day one would supplant the other. All of this comprises a perspective which few of us attain, but one which Clark Gable never lost.

I like to think that this grand old man who Clark Gable first met out there on the pier, together with his beautiful daughter, were there to meet him on November 16, 1960, when he left this world for the next.

LINCOLN, ANGELS AND THE EMANCIPATION PROCLAMATION

Robert M. Webster

(Robert A. Palmer)

(Fall 1948)

A lifelong mystic, Fate co-founder Raymond A. Palmer collected books and clippings about the occult. A great admirer of our sixteenth president, Palmer was particularly interested in the paranormal events that seemed to surround many aspects of Lincoln's life. Among these was one highly important encounter with angels.

THE FOLLOWING reference to Lincoln's Emancipation Proclamation dream comes from his friend Col. Kase, who resided, in 1882, at 1601 North 15th Street, Philadelphia, Pennsylvania.

One night Lincoln dreamed that several angels came to him and called his name. When he answered, asking who they were, they answered:

"We are such as come in God's name for freedom's sake. Behold, millions of His angels look down from heaven, and would come to thy armies, if thou wouldn't but proclaim freedom to the slaves."

Lincoln awoke, much troubled with his dream. The next night the angels came again, re-told their words, and added:

"The great majority of the country is ripe for this matter. Thou fearest this is but a foolish dream. Behold, we will give thee proof tomorrow."

Lincoln awoke more troubled than before.

At that time a seeress named Nettie Mainard lived in Washington. During a séance, attended by Col. Kase, voices spoke to Kase, saying:

"Go, thou, and fetch the president into the presence of this woman."

Kase went to Lincoln and told him what had been said. Lincoln came to see Nettie Mainard, who went into a trance, and the same voices Lincoln had heard in his dream, said:

"We said we would give thee proof tomorrow. Behold, we repeat unto thee, God is in this matter. Save, thou proclaimest the freedom of the slaves, thou shalt not succeed. Do thou this, and the enemy's armies shall melt away like snow in the sun."

Lincoln immediately made his famous Emancipation Proclamation. And true to the angels' words, the armies of the South would soon lay down their arms and go home. The war ended almost miraculously. The slaves were free.

ANGELIC ENCOUNTERS OF PARANORMAL RESEARCHERS

Brad and Sherry Steiger

(Dec. 2008)

Brad Steiger is a most prolific author, researching and writing books on strange and unexplained phenomenon in our time. He and his equally astute wife, Sherry, have had many visitations from angels and other mysterious beings over the years. No better team could be chosen to chronicle heavenly contacts with others who have devoted their lives to investigating the borderlines between the known and the unknown.

A SURVEY released on September 18, 2008, by Baylor University revealed that 55 percent of all adults in the United States (including one in five who stated that they had no religion) believe that they have been protected from harm by a guardian angel.

We thought it would be interesting to query a number of our colleagues in paranormal research and related fields to see if they had ever felt that they had interacted with an angel. We received some very interesting replies from investigators, writers, scientists, and psychics, which we are pleased to share here in our respondents' own words.

Saved from Drowning

PAUL DALE ROBERTS, general manager and ghosthunter of Haunted and Paranormal Investigations International, shared an encounter with an angel that saved his life:

"During the hot summer of 1996, I was with my ex-wife Patricia and her niece at the Sacramento River. We were lying out in the sun and enjoying the water.

"At some point of time, I took the rubber air mattress we had with us and placed it on the calm waters of the river. I was lying on top of the mattress, feeling the warmth of the sun, when a speedboat raced by. The speedboat created high waves, and I found myself falling off the air mattress.

"I was in deep water and found myself sinking quickly. I started panicking. I am not the best swimmer in the world, and before I knew it, I hit bottom.

"Then all of a sudden I felt hands pushing me, grabbing me and pulling me forward towards the shore. As I popped my head out of water, I thought for sure it was my ex-wife who had saved me. Then I looked at the beach area and there was my ex-wife talking with her niece.

"I was shocked. Who was it who had saved me? I looked around to see who my savior was, so I could properly thank my hero. There was no one around to take credit for saving my life. After a while, I was able to swim the rest of the way to shore safely.

"When I got on the beach, I continued to look around for my rescuer. My ex-wife asked what I was looking for. I told her I felt hands and arms grabbing me, pulling me to the shore. When I told her this, she laughed.

"Now, when I think back to this moment, there is only one other logical explanation—it was an angel who saved me. I was saved because it wasn't my time to go. I am to serve another purpose, whatever that purpose may be.

"I believe that we all have guardian angels. They are here to watch us, to observe us, to advise us, to shelter us, to protect us. Embrace your angel, because one day you may need its help."

Miracle Healing

B EVERLY HALE WATSON is a minister and the author of 30 inspirational books. She is also the founder and director of the Sevenfold Peace Foundation in Grapevine, Texas, which offers intuitive counseling, educational materials, classes and support services to individuals on the path to enlightenment. The Foundation also works with local community service agencies in providing assistance to people coping with serious life challenges.

Beverly's encounter with an angel resulted in a dramatic miracle healing:

"Hospitalized at the age of 24 for possible breast cancer, I was scheduled for surgery early the next morning. In order to divert my mind from the surgery, I was preparing a Sunday school lesson at approximately 11:15 P.M. All of a sudden I realized that my life was totally in God's hands.

"I started to pray and said, 'Thy will be done!' Instantly an angel appeared at the foot of my bed. It was a brilliant Light Being (like the sun) that went from the floor to ceiling and the width of the bed. As it faced me, great love poured forth from the angel. At the same time a surge of heat entered the crown of my head, shot through my body, and exited my feet, leaving me with a peace that passes all understanding.

"I was wheeled into surgery at 8:00 A.M. the next morning. When the doctors opened me up they found nothing—not even what had appeared on the x-rays. All tumors and cysts were gone. I had received a miracle healing.

"Three weeks later, I realized that I had been blessed with unexplainable spiritual 'gifts' to be used to help mankind. Thus began my life's journey in service to God."

Angelic Physician

PASTOR ROBIN SWOPE has written about a personal encounter that he had with an angelic being while pastoring a Christian and Missionary Alliance church in New Castle, Pennsylvania, in his blog article, "Angels of Mercy." For this article, he has retold a remarkable angelic encounter that one of his parishioners experienced:

"Debbie was almost to term with her baby when she was called out to work. It was time for rush hour traffic, and she took small side roads through the mountains to get to the city. On a narrow curve, she lost control of her car and it tumbled down the small hill off the side of the road.

"Luckily the crash was buffered by landing on the limbs of the trees that littered the side of the hill, but still it was bad enough. Debbie had broken her leg in the crash. But she took a deep breath, regained her composure, and fashioned a makeshift tourniquet to stop the bleeding. She flipped open her cell phone and called 911.

"When asked by the operator where exactly she was, Debbie had no clue. Unfortunately this was the early 1990s and at that time they did not have our modern GPS equipment that we use to find stranded motorists. Back then many crash victims would call 911 to ask for help only to let the operator hear them slowly die from their injuries. Having friends in the health care field she knew these stories all too well.

"That was when the panic set in. She knew the search parties sent to look for her could pass by on the road above and not even know she was there.

"She tried to drag herself from the wreckage so she could make it to the road above. But in the struggle her water broke.

"Lying there in pain and panic, a man appeared. He had a medical bag in his hand and immediately got to work in silence.

"Once the baby was delivered and Debbie's wounds were set, they made their way up the cliff to the road above.

"Resting at the top on the guardrail, Debbie saw the oncoming lights of the sheriff's van come across the turn.

"She turned to thank her rescuer, but he had vanished into nowhere."

Crystals and Frozen Pipes

LORI JEAN FLORY is the author of the bestselling *The Wisdom Teachings of Archangel Michael* (1997) and is highly respected as a teacher and counselor. Although she has experienced many miracles, she chose to recount an angelic interaction that dealt with the rather mundane problem of frozen water pipes:

"Years ago, it must have been the early '90s, Denver had a lengthy winter cold snap of temperatures well below zero. I was working as a travel agent at the time, and while my ex-husband Charles and I had been to work one day, we had accidentally forgotten to let hot water drip in the pipes. Well, you guessed it, the pipes were frozen when we got home that night. I remember Charles getting on the phone when we got home, trying to call plumbers to help. So many had the same problem at that time, that all that could be done initially was to leave a voice mail for the plumbing service.

"It came time to go to bed, and I lay on the bed holding a favorite cluster of quartz crystals on my solar plexus. I was affirming 'I AM the presence of all angelic resource and abundance. I AM God presence. Go forth and do this now.' Over and over I affirmed this.

"As I meditated, a sudden flash of light appeared above me. In that same second, the cluster of quartz crystals on my solar plexus literally and physically fell apart. Accompanied by the angelic light, the crystals fell in a clean break into four separate crystals, just as if a laser beam had cut them apart in that second. I know that a molecular shift took place in that moment, associated with that divine light. Charles saw the light as well. It was not only myself.

"Right after that, even though it was well below zero outside, Charles got up and went to the bathroom and turned on hot water! And the pipes did not break. All of a sudden we had hot water back.

"At the same time the phone rang. It was the plumber, and Charles was able to tell him that we no longer needed help. You can bet we did not forget to let the hot water drip in the pipes again.

"I still have the crystals that fell apart from that cluster. I have always kept them with me."

Angel's Wing

NORMA JOINER is a paranormal researcher and student of the ancient and traditional teachings of the Polynesian Kahuna. Her website emphasizes mystical teachings of Native Americans and her native Hawaii:

"My encounter happened during the early 1980s at a time when I was searching and becoming intrigued with that strong sense of something else happening to me. I was involved with various group gatherings and was finding my way through meditation and understanding the art of being quiet and listening.

"I would sit at a specific time and be quiet. It was usually in the bedroom with the door closed, a dim lamp on, and sitting in the middle of the room on the carpet. I would face west, and off to the left of me was a floor-to-ceiling louvered window.

"I would always start off singing my mantra; however, that night I felt different, and I sat and closed my eyes. It was very quiet.

"Then I began to feel warm, and I sensed that the room had gotten very bright (I could see it even though my eyes were closed) and I heard a ruffled sound.

"I began to turn my head towards the left . . . it was like a slow motion feeling . . . and just as I turned and opened my eyes I felt a breeze and something touched my left cheek. I opened my eyes and the light was very bright, and I saw a large white wing with feathers by the window . . . something I had never seen before. I couldn't move, and I kept looking at the window as the wing disappeared and the bright light became the dim light from the lamp.

"I sat for a long time waiting and I felt warm all over and I knew that something had been there. It wasn't very long after that, that I encountered the Archangel Michael . . . and that's another story."

Vanishing Truck

PATRICIA RESS is a newspaper reporter, magazine writer, novelist, and radio host who has explored the paranormal for many years. She, too, has had her own encounter with an angel:

"Several years ago my husband and I were going through a spate of financial hard luck. Nothing dire, just hard on us.

"One night we had both been working extra hours. My husband picked me up after work and we were heading home in one of our older, unreliable cars. About halfway home, our car engine went out at a stop sign, and we had no idea how we could get help at that hour.

"I was beside myself when out of nowhere a huge, white pickup pulled up behind us with a hook and chain and offered to pull us home. We agreed and he did.

71

"When we got home, we told the man to wait a moment as we had to open the house and make sure everything was all right. But when we went back out into the driveway, he and his huge white truck were gone.

"He couldn't possibly have left that quickly or manipulated his large truck out of the area where he had pulled us in front of our kitchen door. To this day, we believe that this was somehow an angel and it was a message that God was indeed watching over us.

"And as a kicker to this angel incident, I turned on the radio to get ready for bed, and they were playing a song called *Angels Among Us*."

Copper Pyramid

WHO SAYS that scientists cannot be touched by angels? This medical researcher admits that he has received contact with angelic teachers for over 60 years.

Dr. C. Norman Shealy, M.D., Ph.D., is well known worldwide as an innovative healer and teacher. He is Professor of Energy Medicine and President Emeritus of Holos University Graduate Seminary, and this is his story:

"For over 60 years I have had sudden important 'knowings,' sometimes as a vision, sometimes as an abstract understanding. Twenty-four years ago I experienced the first of a few dozen audible contacts with angelic guides. One of the most important took place about 16 years ago, while I was jogging in the woods in Holland. I suddenly had a vision of a copper pyramid with crystals at the top. I made a sketch of this when I returned to my room. The following night my angelic teacher spoke to me: 'Where do you think that image came from yesterday?'

"I replied: 'I thought it was mine.' My guide said: 'I put it there. You need to work with that.'

"I returned home and received permission to work with 75 patients in such a pyramid, activated by a Tesla coil. I treated them daily for one hour, five days a week, for two weeks, 25 patients, each with rheumatoid arthritis, back pain, or depression. Seventy percent were markedly improved within two weeks.

"But I felt there was no way to get this device approved by the FDA. So for the next 12 years I worked with five other circuits in the human body, developed a specific stimulator, the SheLi TENS, which could reduce pain, as well as selectively raise DHEA (dehydroepiandrosterone), aldosterone, neurotensin, or calcitonin, or reduce free radicals.

"The guide gave me the physical locations of points; I had to figure out the proper acupuncture points and the neurochemistry. That done, I came to the conclusion that life could be extended to an average of 140 years if people would just activate at least the three energetic rings to rejuvenate DHEA and calcitonin as well as reduce free radicals. I presented this work in my book *Life Beyond 100: Secret of the Fountain.*

"As I spoke in over 42 cities about this approach, I learned that a majority of people were not willing to spend 20 minutes a day required for the work. And in fact, a majority of people were not interested in living even to 100 years!

"In January 2007, I awoke at 4:00 A.M. with the image of that copper pyramid, and knew I had not finished the work given to me years earlier. I then tested the effect of the pyramid on telomere rejuvenation in six volunteers. Telomeres are the tail of DNA and are an accurate reflection of longevity. Ordinarily telomeres shrink an average of one percent each year. Within three months telomeres had regrown an average of one percent.

"As I talked about this I learned that most people would not put a pyramid in their house. After careful meditation, I realized that the only way this finding might be useful was to convert it to a mattress pad.

"Integrating another message from 20 years ago—'If you placed crushed sapphire over the heart, it would bypass the need for bypass surgery'—I created the mattress pad with copper and sapphire, connected to a Tesla coil. This can then be plugged into a timer, so that the entire solar homeopathic treatment (a term given me by the angelic guide) can be done while you sleep.

"Within an additional seven months on this device, the six subjects had had telomeres grow an average of 2.9 percent. This means that rejuvenation of telomeres is proceeding at an average of 3.4 percent each year, instead of declining at one percent per year.

"I have applied for a patent on this approach. It will be my 11th patent. All have been the result of angelic guidance!

"Indeed, I consider my entire career guided by angelic wisdom.

"I have documented much of my 85 percent successful therapeutic approach in over 30,000 patients in a DVD, *Medical Renaissance: The Secret Code.*"

Ask for Angels' Help

CLARISA BERNHARDT is one of today's leading psychics, who first came to national attention because of the accuracy of her predictions regarding earthquakes. The "Earthquake Lady" soon became popular as a psychic to Hollywood stars and celebrities, and in one dramatic instance, may have been instrumental in saving the life of

President Gerald Ford. Clarisa also writes an astrological column for Shirley MacLaine's website. Clarisa is widely recognized for her mediumistic abilities and her regular angelic communications.

Clarisa shared the following:

"As the Christmas holiday season comes full circle in this beautiful time of the year, it bestows an extra needed sparkle of good will in the heart of many individuals. It is also a time when the ethereal presence of angels' energy seems to prevail everywhere, which is easily felt as they gently command a place in one's thoughts.

"One of my angelic communications expressed to me the importance for people to be aware that they are not limited to this time of the year and can appear with a message anywhere or at any moment.

"In a beautiful vision, the angels also told me they so want to help people, but they must be asked. Usually after a brief message they are gone. However, on this occasion they lingered. Then stepped forward to me and said they were surprised more people did not ask for help.

"From then on I have tried to let people know that the angels truly want to help, but there seems to be an important divine rule that they must be asked.

"You are helping angels fulfill their destiny by asking them for help. You can help angels by communicating with them, simply speaking softly as you see them in your heart. Have no doubt, they will try to help you as they are allowed.

"I feel blessed to have received several communications on numerous occasions from the archangel Raphael. Earlier this year the archangel gave me a message that might be encouraging to others in seemingly difficult times such as the world is currently experiencing. He usually speaks to me of Hope, and I would like to share this message now with you:"

A Message from the Archangel, Raphael, given to Clarisa Bernhardt, May 2008.

When you find Hope; embrace it with the inner
Starlight of your heart—
As you walk towards the dawn of a new day.
For Hope carries one through the darkest of nights and times to the
Brightness of a morning filled with shining new possibilities!
If you are looking for something beautiful to give another,
Then simply try giving them hope, and you will find that you
Have also given it to yourself!

PART III

ANGELIC ENCOUNTERS
HAPPEN TO EVERYONE

*F*OR MORE THAN *six decades Fate readers and contributors have been writing in to share their own personal stories of encounters with heavenly visitants. Men and women from every walk of life and every corner of the globe have come face to face with angels in time of need. What follows is a small sampling of the testimony the magazine has received.*

MY EXPERIENCES WITH ANGELS AND OTHER METAPHYSICAL MYSTERIES

Melodee K. Currier
(Dec. 2012)

Melodee Currier is a widely published author on many subjects; she has had a lifelong fascination with metaphysics and has studied it extensively. She is alive to the angels around her and walks and speaks with her own, on a daily basis.

FOR AS LONG as I can remember, our family's conversations centered around ESP, ghosts, and many other metaphysical mysteries. Early memories include my mother and her sister, living in different cities, sending and receiving mental messages to each other at a specific time of the day. One psychic game we'd play in our family was to take a deck of playing cards, have one person look at a card and ask others to say what color suit the card is. I remember closing my eyes and actually seeing the color red if the suit was diamonds or hearts. I was able to guess the color of the suit correctly most of the time. So it's not surprising that paranormal is my normal.

Major paranormal experiences began when I was a teenager and they have continued over the years. Some happenings were minor, but some, including seeing an angel, were awesome. I have briefly described the major ones below. They are all factual and I've listed them in order as they happened.

1. My first psychic experience occurred while on a blind date. My date turned out to be boring and disappointing. I had nothing to lose, so I decided to spice things up and tell him all about himself—from how many fillings he had in his mouth to his brother's middle name. I was 100-percent correct, and it totally freaked him out.

2. An angel gave me a message when I was 25. My father was in the hospital with a terminal illness. My mother and I would take turns visiting him at the hospital every other day. One evening after my visit, I called my mother to tell her that he wasn't doing well that day. After going to sleep that night I was awakened at 11:00 P.M. by three very loud knocks and a male voice that said very slowly "He . . . is . . . gone." I mentally replied, "No . . . it's too soon." and went back to sleep. At midnight my mother

called me from the hospital. My father had died at 11:00 P.M., the time the angel told me he was gone.

3. I love to attend psychic workshops and was attending a spirit guide workshop when something very shocking happened. It was during a meditation to meet our female spirit guides. When mine wasn't responding, I mentally said "*Please* give me a sign!" With that, she practically shoved me off my chair. I was stunned and thrilled at the same time. Tears came to my eyes and the instructor could see that something had happened and asked me to share it with the class.

4. Before we had cell phones, whenever I had a car problem, my car was always miraculously "driven" right to a pay phone or a safe place, like a parking lot. I always said a prayer of thankfulness and my luck continued.

5. Once when I was watching the news on TV, the neighbor of a man who had been killed was being interviewed by a reporter. The first thing that came to my mind was—*he* did it. A couple days later I saw on the news that he had been the one who killed his neighbor.

6. During a shopping trip, I had the strong feeling that someone was shoplifting near me. I looked around and also saw a man I believed to be an undercover cop.

I went to the counter and told the clerk my suspicions. She confirmed that he was an undercover cop and she let him know about the shoplifter. My instincts proved to be accurate.

7. The first time I heard the "radio" I was trying to go to sleep, but it sounded as though someone was playing music and having a party nearby. So I got up and walked through my apartment to see if I could find where the sound was coming from—but the radio kept following me. Wherever I went, there it was. I couldn't figure it out so I went back to bed and fell asleep. In the nights that followed, before I went to sleep, I frequently heard that radio sound. About a year later I moved from Florida to Ohio. My first night sleeping in my new apartment, I heard the radio. Sometimes it would be music I had never heard before and sometimes I would hear talking. Once I tried to decipher what the words were and I heard "They are Americans." At this point, I was hearing the radio either as I was waking up or before I went to sleep, sometimes twice a day. It eventually became annoying, so I asked it to leave. The next day I didn't hear the radio. And it did not return until a couple months later when I decided to invite it back. Eventually it left again and I haven't heard the radio for over 20 years.

8. For several months after my mother died I was frequently visited by a very unusual smell. One day while my husband I were driving on the

expressway I smelled a similar scent and asked him what it was. He said it smelled to him like a crematorium. My mother was cremated and it then made sense that she came to me in the form of that smell.

One morning at 5:00 A.M. I opened my eyes -- shocked to see an angel hovering over me. She had medium length, sandy blonde hair, wore a full length aqua and gold robe and had large white wings. I surprised her by opening my eyes at that hour and the second she realized I saw her she disappeared like a bubble bursting. I wasn't scared, but in awe and exclaimed, "*Wow!*"

9. A few years ago during a visit to a psychic, I mentioned to her I was planning to sign up for her psychic development classes. She replied that I didn't need her classes, I was already there. She also said I was a medium and could channel and she advised me to get my business cards printed and start giving readings.

10. I recently read a book regarding Archangel Rafael. It stated he is the archangel relating to health matters and you will know he is there by the color emerald green. A couple days later I felt very ill. I held my head in my hands with my eyes closed and prayed to Archangel Rafael to help me. When I opened my eyes for about two seconds everything was the color emerald green. I instantly knew Archangel Rafael was there and answering my prayers and my symptoms disappeared immediately. I also had another occasion to pray to Archangel Rafael to help me with a health matter and he instantly helped me then as well.

11. This morning my husband and I had breakfast at a local restaurant. There was a table of six people at the other end of the room, with one woman speaking very loudly about dogs and monopolizing the conversation. I quietly said to my husband, "Some people are like that. They talk all the time." Instantly I heard the woman say, "Some people are like that. They talk all the time." She repeated the *exact* words I had just said to my husband about her. It was surreal! If my husband hadn't been there to hear it, I would have sworn I imagined it.

12. Some experiences I've had on a smaller scale include: On occasion I've heard my husband call my name (although he didn't actually call it) and have him appear at that very moment. When I was temping as a secretary for a woman who was on maternity leave, I heard her in labor at the same time she was having her baby. Driving home after a job interview I heard a voice say "The job is yours." And soon after I was offered the job. When I was single, I made a list of attributes I wanted in a future husband and recited them out loud to the universe. Within a very short period of time, I met my husband who possessed 95 percent of those attributes.

WHO SAVED US?

Judith Oehler
(Sept. 2013)

A longtime FATE *reader shares her own experience with a heavenly presence. A big-rig truck was barreling straight toward her in her own lane while passing a car. Then she heard a voice say something shocking.*

CLEANING out the refrigerator after a summer at the cottage was a challenging activity. Where did the time go? Here we were packing up, cleaning and loading the car for the drive back to Jersey. We had one more stop to make at the vet's to get a check-up for our pets. Around 4 o'clock we were on our way.

I drove down the old Gull Bay Road to connect with Highway 22. The view was clear, the day bright and there was little traffic on the road. I turned right and began to move forward when I heard my husband, John, yell "stop" in a panicked voice.

I slammed on the brakes and looked around, bewildered. Off in the far distance I saw a big-rig cab in our lane, passing a car. I thought there wouldn't be a problem as all I needed to do was pull over to the shoulder if it didn't get in its own lane by the time it reached us. Then it happened!

A sense of calm seemed to come over us. I felt as if I was in a dream-like state. Mentally I told myself to move over or back the car up as I was only a few feet from Gull Bay Road.

Instead I heard a woman's voice say, "This is your death. You are going to die." I couldn't believe my ears.

I thought to myself *Really? By that thing barreling down the road at us?* At this point the rig was accelerating in its attempt to pass the little tan car and it was still coming at us head on.

I put my hands on the wheel and in a kind of stupor looked at it as it rapidly approached. John also sat unconcerned and said nothing. There was no sense of fear or hysterics. We calmly sat there and waited for the impact.

I couldn't take my eyes off the approaching van. I thought to myself: *What a mess this is going to be. Too bad the pets are on board. My, it's taking a long time for this thing to come. Hey, we've got air bags. That should save us, shouldn't it? I wonder what everybody will say when they get the news. Well, here it comes—good-bye world!*

Now if that doesn't make you want to ask a few questions this next happening will. I became aware of another woman outside our vehicle on the right front side of the fender. I sensed she was middle-aged, tough and a little bit dumpy. There was a conversation going on between these two females, and, while I couldn't make out what was said in its entirety, I caught snatches of it. "Murder?" she asked. "Him too?"

"Not a hair on his head," the older lady said.

The sound of the big green cab was deafening now. I saw the chrome bumper clearly, no more than 100 feet in front of us. A putrid stench of burning rubber filled my senses and I was stunned to see a blue-grey cloud envelop us. The rig disappeared, only to appear no more than a few feet or so from us. It was sliding into its own lane.

Again I'm thinking *it's not going to make it. We're as good as dead. Look, it missed John's side of the car but it will clip my side and spin us around.*

I couldn't stand the smell.

It was like watching "slo-mo" on the TV. I held my breath as the monster truck roared past us with only inches to spare. This couldn't possibly be real, I mused. Is this all my imagination or am I really sitting in the middle of the highway with the car idling while an oversized trailer cab just skidded around us?

"Okay, you can go now," said the middle-aged, tough spirit from out of nowhere.

I put my foot on the accelerator and slowly began to gain speed. I was numb, and in shock. How could I still be alive?

Who was that entity that saved us? I glanced over at John and he said nothing.

The next day I was still shaken and traumatized. I paced around, couldn't sleep, function or respond. I went over and over the details in my mind wondering how I could just sit there calmly and curiously watch that vehicle come, knowing the outcome.

Finally, I felt the need to do something to get myself together. I ordered myself outside to do some gardening. As I raked and dug in the earth I became aware of that presence again. Let me ask you how you feel about guardians . . . . Halos? Angelic countenance? Wings maybe? How about comfort from the heavenly realm?

None of that kind of thing applied to my situation. This feisty spiritual being spoke directly to me saying, "Quit your whining, you're not going to die!"

So that's my story.

I'm on the mend psychologically, but am still a little nervous about driving on long trips.

You can say what you want about this spiritual benefactor but I guess I should be grateful. Oh how I wish I could just hug this dear old lady from the other side, whoever she may be.

WHERE IS OUR HELP?

Gwen Beck
(As told to Margaret K. Look)
(Dec. 2003)

Angels appear to help people in the oddest places at the oddest times. But always when they are most needed. In the middle of nowhere, in the middle of a deserted rest stop, one appeared out of nowhere to help a Montana woman and her husband.

I'LL ALWAYS REMEMBER the fall of 1988, because God sent an angel in answer to my call for help.

My husband Cecil was a very sick man, He had retired in 1975 due to poor health after 40 years of teaching industrial arts. He had emphysema and poor circulation in his legs.

We had made many trips to Billings, Montana, a hundred miles from our home in Powell, Wyoming, to get medical care for him. First, he had vein transplants in his legs, then had his right leg amputated.

Cec, as everyone called him, was a very courageous man, a loving and kind man, who was never bitter about his situation. He was determined, at age 75, to walk with a prosthesis. And he did.

By 1988, Cec had lost his second leg, then became seriously ill with a stomach disorder. He had to see the doctors in Billings. On this bright October day, I was loading the car with oxygen tanks, an oxygenator, suitcases, jackets, canes, crutches, medication, and whatever we thought we might need on this trip, when our minister, Maurie Campbell, and several friends arrived to help. They also assisted Cec in getting from his wheelchair to the front seat of the car.

"Let's join hands and pray," Maurie said. He asked God to be with us all the way to Billings and to guide the doctors in their care of Cec. We thanked everyone, then went on our way.

When we were about 15 miles from Billings, near Laurel, Montana, our worst fears were realized. Cec became ill and had to get to a restroom. I had no idea where I could take him. Many of the gas stations were not adapted for a man in a wheelchair.

Then I saw a campground. It looked deserted, but we decided to take a chance that the restroom was still open.

In my anxiety I drove past the door. I hurried to get the wheelchair out of the trunk of the car. Then, with Cec helping by pushing on his one prosthesis, we got him into the wheelchair. It was a struggle. Then we had to get the wheelchair through the gravel that covered the ground to the restroom. We got there, and it was open. "Praise the Lord," I said.

I wheeled Cec into the booth for the handicapped, and with his help, I got him on the toilet. Then I could not get him off, because I couldn't lift him.

What was I going to do? His doctor's appointment was at one o'clock.

I went to the outer area of the restroom. "Oh, God, where is our help?" I prayed desperately. "I can't lift him. He weighs 200 pounds and has no legs. Where is the help we prayed for?"

As I was finishing this prayer, a man stepped into the doorway of the restroom. He appeared to be in his 50s, of medium height, with gray hair and a gray beard. He had soft blue eyes and was wearing blue, well-worn, western work clothes. He seemed so clean—his clothes, his hair—everything about him was clean and fresh.

I started to explain why I was there. He just walked right by me, as if he knew where Cec was. He said, "I can help you."

He lifted my husband into the wheelchair, then, looking at me, said, "I will take him out for you."

After he put Cec in the front seat, he wrapped his arms around him and said, "Jesus loves you. Things look bad now, but they're going to get better, because Jesus is going to help you. Remember, Jesus loves you."

As he was loading the wheelchair into the trunk of the car, I told him, "God sent you to help us."

He explained that he had lost his job on a ranch in Montana and was hitchhiking to Amarillo, Texas. "I'm going to need some help to get there," he added.

I looked around the deserted campground, noticing that there were no other cars there and that this man did not have a backpack or a suitcase.

"Could I give you ten dollars? Would this help you in any way?" I asked.

"Yes, it would," he replied.

When I got into the car, Cec asked, "Did you give him 20 dollars?"

"No, Honey, I gave him ten."

"Give him ten more dollars," Cec told me.

I took another ten dollar bill from my purse and, reaching across Cec to the man who was standing by the passenger side of the car, gave it to him.

He put his arms around Cec again, gave him a big hug, and said, "Jesus loves you. Remember, things are going to get better?'

"We've been praying," I said.

"You keep on praying," the man urged, as he shut the car door.

We started to thank him, but he disappeared. He was no place in the campground.

"How could he disappear so fast?" Cec asked, astonished.

"God sent us an angel to help us in answer to our prayers," I said.

Still looking around for the man, Cec said, "I've never met a man so strong. He lifted me as if I were a rag doll."

We were on time for our appointment in Billings. The doctor prescribed medication for Cec's stomach problems, enabling him to eat a hearty breakfast the next morning, the first real meal he had had in a long time.

Later, when I described our experience to the children in my Bible Study Group, a boy said, "You had to give him the 20 dollars, because there was somebody somewhere who needed the money"

"Yes. The angel is busy helping people in need," I said.

This experience convinced Cec that God would always take care of him. It helped him live triumphantly through physical setbacks until his peaceful death on November 24, 1991. I feel sure his angel escorted him home to be with our Heavenly Father.

MY HEALING ANGEL

Charlie R. Brown

(July 2009)

The healing powers of our heavenly visitors have been sung since the dawn of history. Reader Charlie R. Brown's experience with an angel manifesting such abilities could stand in for the experiences with millions, perhaps billions, of other people in similar circumstances.

I HAD JUST ARRIVED at church on Easter Sunday, where I was scheduled to deliver the sermon. There were people behind me that I did not know. As I entered the church, one of the members called to me, "Charlie Brown, it's about time you got here." I was 15 minutes early, but they had expected me sooner.

A few minutes later, I was approached by a man who came up behind me. He asked if I was the same Charlie Brown that writes about angels. I told him I didn't know if I was the only one, but I did write about angels.

"Did you write one about 50 years ago about your brother?" he asked.

I paused in amazement. "Yes, I did," I replied. I had totally forgotten the story. It appeared in a magazine that I could no longer remember.

"I am Jimmy Ledbetter," the man told me. "I was with you when you shot your brother with the arrow. We were playing cowboys and Indians. You accidentally shot your brother in the eye." He paused in reflection.

As I walked up to the podium, I was taken back 50 years. It had been Easter Sunday when we were playing in the woods behind our home. I was 13. My two younger brothers and I were playing with Jimmy at our fortified cave about a mile behind our farm home. My brothers were soldiers defending the fort. Jimmy and I were attacking Indians with homemade bows and spears fashioned from local willow trees. We would shoot our arrows and when we ran out, we called a truce to retrieve them. No one expected anyone to get hurt. My last arrow struck my younger brother in the eye. Bobby started screaming and everyone panicked.

Religion was a daily practice in our household. I would even say my family was one of the worst examples of holy rollers that I had ever seen. My father drank and often came home drunk. My mother would continually pray that he would not come home in a crazed frenzy. We attended church every Sunday. We missed that Sunday because I was just getting over chicken pox: a reprieve for one Sunday out of 52.

I had always been impressed by the power of prayer. There was always someone who declared health problems or other maladies had been healed through prayer. I witnessed a crippled man throw down his crutches and walk, independent of any assistance.

"Gather around him" I shouted. "We have got to pray for him."

At 13, I wasn't too sure of how to pray. I was accustomed to church members jumping, shouting, and speaking in tongues. We placed our hands on Bobby and prayed the Lord's Prayer. I picked him up with the assistance of my other brother, Floyd. We started running up the hill to the highway. Old Doctor Coffey lived about half a mile away. We headed for his house.

Fortunately a neighbor stopped and drove us to his door. It was probably an hour before we got there. Mom and Dad were taking food to a sick friend and we could not reach them.

All the way, Bobby kept screaming that he could not see. I prayed all the way to the doctor and while he was being examined. I could hear the doctor trying to appease him. Nothing the doctor could say would help. The doctor cleaned the blood and came out to see me.

"Where did the blood come from?" he asked.

"It came from his eye where I shot him with an arrow," I replied.

The doctor scratched his head in total confusion. "There are signs of broken blood vessels in his eye, but no injury that would produce that amount of blood. Are you sure you hit him with an arrow?"

"Of course I did," I said. "I saw him pull the arrow out."

Finally Bobby settled down. The doctor kept telling him that there was no wound and that he was not blind.

We didn't have any money and the doctor said, "Well, I didn't have to sew him up, so I guess there is no charge." In those days, most of his house calls were paid for in kind. Few people had enough money for food. Doctor bills were unheard of. Unless we were bleeding to death, no one went to a doctor.

We began the trek back home. Bobby asked, "Who was the person who kept his hand on my eye while we were going to the doctor?"

I told him that no one held his eye. We were too busy simply getting him back to the main road.

"No," he replied. "Someone was beside me all the way to the doctor with his hand over my eye." He described a tall, glowing man dressed all in white.

"It must have been a healing angel," I told him. I felt cold chills run down my spine. This was a miracle and I was part of it.

I had heard of healing angels all my life. I had witnessed many healings in church. We even had roving preachers who would go house to house administering to the sick. Many of the bedridden would get out of bed, totally cured without the aid of a physician. I suppose that was why I was consumed by the urge to become an administrator for God.

This was 50 years ago to the day. The minister of the church, Margaret Ann Schmidt, had no idea that when she asked me to do the Easter Sunday sermon that it would be the culmination of a 50-year-old prayer.

As children, we think as children and act as children. When we are older, we put away childish things. Well maybe, just maybe, we shouldn't.

THE DOG THAT DISAPPEARED

Mai Packwood
(Nov. 1956)

Angelic visitors take many forms from glowing light to ethereal human beings to winged presences. One Fate reader reported that hers appeared in canine guise.

THE STRANGEST thing I've ever experienced happened to me in February, 1928, when my second child, Verne, was three weeks old. My first girl was nearing her third birthday. My husband, Tom, worked nights, usually getting home around 2:15 A.M. My mornings were spent keeping the babies quiet so he could get his rest and for the most part my household tasks had to be done at night.

It was not unusual for me to be either hanging out or bringing in the wash near midnight. This February night I was bringing in the wash at a little past 11:00 P.M. I heard the lock on the kitchen door snap shut behind me with a very loud click. I was conscious of the click because I was not in the habit of locking the door. I went in and out regularly and I was not afraid despite the many warnings of my neighbors about locking my doors at night. Now the click of the back door seemed an ominous reminder to me that I had not locked the front door either.

The stillness that engulfed the house was something I had never felt before. Somehow the very air seemed to be saying that something was about to happen. I set my laundry basket down in the bedroom where my two babies slept peacefully. I noticed the baby acted a little restless. Three-year-old Nita suddenly opened her eyes and looked around as if in fright. Seeing me standing so near she was reassured and went back to sleep.

At that very instant I heard the heavy growl of an angry dog. The growling grew louder and I could hear a vicious gnashing of the teeth now too. It had to be a big dog! This shocked me as we owned no dog. There were only a few dogs in our neighborhood, all of them rather small house pets.

I looked through a crack in the front door blind and from my darkened room could see, to my consternation, the biggest dog I could ever imagine. His muscles were tense; he was crouched ready to spring. In the light from the streetlamp I could see his hackles standing high on his shoulders and neck. Then I saw that he was growling his warning to an approaching intruder. A man was inching his way up my front steps.

I could not see the man's face but everything about him spelled danger and destruction. For the first time in my life I felt fear, a deep, terrifying fear. At that moment the man put his foot on the top step and suddenly the dog was upon him. For a brief instant there was wild fury as the man and beast rolled together down the stairs. Then the man let out a scream, wrenched himself free, and ran in panic down the street. The dog calmly walked back up onto the porch and lay down with his back to the door. His muzzle rested on his front paws as he watched the man vanish.

I was able to move once more and I turned the key in the front door lock. I wanted to go out and pet the dog but fear would not let me.

When Tom came home at the usual hour he asked me where I got the dog. He had seen it when he turned into the driveway. I told him of my terrifying experience as I put the steak I had just cooked on his supper plate.

Before he would take a bite Tom had to go out and see the dog. We both stroked his head. and he received the petting. My husband remarked that he never had seen such a huge dog. He thought we ought to try to keep him and we both hoped he would stay. Tom went back into the house and brought out his supper steak and set it before the dog who made no effort to touch it, only looking up at us with friendly eyes.

Next morning Tom got up early but the dog was gone and so was the steak.

Hoping to find the dog in the neighborhood we spent most of the morning driving around looking for him anxiously. We inquired as we looked but no one had seen such a dog. Everyone raised their eyebrows skeptically when we described his size.

We never saw the dog again. I felt that something great had passed my way unexpectedly.

When the evening paper came I knew from what the dog had saved us. On the front page was the account of the recapture of an escaped, criminally insane man. The authorities had been searching for him for several days and had picked him up near midnight less than a mile from our home. He had deep lacerations about his neck and shoulders, which he claimed he got from a dog, big as a yearling. The authorities discredited his story about the dog's size but would give him rabies shots nevertheless, the story said.

ANGEL IN A PINCH

Maia Geikie

(June 1990)

Another reader reported the opposite experience. An angelic presence came into her life to save her family's dearly beloved dog.

HAVE YOU EVER entertained or been entertained by an angel, unawares? The question is not so unlikely as you may suppose. In 1984 a book entitled A *Handbook of Angels* by H. C. was translated from Dutch into English and immediately made the rounds of various occult fraternities in Britain. The author had been prompted to write the book by a sermon given in Leiden in 1981 in which the minister called angels "a forgotten group." Dr. Moolenburgh began his research with some 400 of his own patients, asking each if they believed in angels, and if they had ever seen or had contact with an angel. The result was both spectacular and surprising—the latter because many reported sightings were of angels dressed in everyday clothes.

After reading *A Handbook of Angels,* I began to wonder about an extraordinary experience of my own and, indirectly, of my family, which had occurred some years ago. I feel certain that the manifestation witnessed at that time could only have been that of an angel. We have often discussed the phenomenon among ourselves, yet it never occurred to us that we may have been helped by an angel—until now—although we *had* realized our helper was not someone of this world.

Bad Weather for a Vacation

IT HAPPENED some 13 years ago while we were vacationing in Wester Ross. Our group consisted of my husband Ian, our daughter Mary and her boyfriend Andy, two large standard poodles and myself.

As a holiday it hadn't been a howling success because the weather was more fitting for ducks than dogs and humans. Our cottage near Mellon Charles had a leaky roof, necessitating an assortment of buckets and bowls stationed along the landing to catch the drips, and at the same time providing booby traps for anyone dashing along to the bathroom in the dark. Eventually we gave up and moved to a hotel in Aultbea.

One day we drove to the headland at Wester Ross through horizontal rain and drifting mist as this seemed more interesting than watching rain through our hotel windows. We parked near the headland just beyond the village of Cove because the dogs indicated they wanted to be let out. Mary and Andy volunteered to escort them while Ian and I stayed in the car, a suggestion we promptly accepted since the car was warm and snug while outside the elements were having themselves a whale of a time.

We settled down with books and papers while the younger generation and canines braved the weather. Five minutes later Mary violently wrenched the door open. Trying to make herself heard above the yowling wind, she screamed at me, "Come quickly, Mummy, Jo has run over the edge of the cliff and fallen into the sea!"

That was the gist of the message, although at the time it wasn't so clearly articulated. Earlier I had taken off my shoes and now had difficulty getting them on again, so without further ado I chased after Mary in stockinged feet.

JoJo (more often called "Jo"), the younger of the two poodles, had, in carefree abandon, charged across the springy grass. The mist was dense at the top of the head land, and by the time she had sensed the hidden cliff edge, it was too late. She skidded but was unable to stop, and had pitched over the edge into the angry sea below.

100 Feet Below Us, JoJo Was on a Ledge of Death

A SMALL KNOT of spectators had materialized out of the mist and were gathered around Andy who was explaining, "The tide flung her onto the rocks and she's just this minute managed to claw her way on to that ledge." He pointed to a spot 100 feet below us where Jo sat on a narrow strip of rocky terrain, howling her head off.

From where we stood, her face looked to be quite bloody. The small, narrow horseshoe-shaped inlet afforded her some shelter from the worst of the weather, but the situation was bad.

There were about five or six people on our side and a similar number on the opposite edge of the horseshoe. Everyone was shouting at once, offering their advice. Those on the opposite side might just as well have saved their breath as we couldn't hear a word above the uproar of the elements. I called down to Jo repeatedly, but it was obvious she couldn't hear me.

Having done a little rock climbing in my youth, I decided to try and reach Jo. Finding what looked like a promising place I ventured to descend, but after some seven or eight feet I became hopelessly stuck. The rock face sheered steeply inwards making further descent impossible without a rope, so I climbed back to the top.

With the howling dog below, the screaming wind and the report of the sea—sounding just like a gun being fired as it hit the rocks—it seemed as if all hell had let loose and we became more and more desperate.

The Weather Worsens

THE WEATHER worsened and our onlookers gradually drifted away, but not without words of encouragement and more hopeless advice. They seemed to be just as concerned for JoJo as we were.

Something urgent had to be done. It was decided that Mary and Andy should take the car and drive to the village in hopes of finding a fisherman intrepid enough to brave the turbulent waves and take a boat around the headland to rescue Jo—a forlorn hope, but worth a try. My husband thought that someone *somewhere* must have a length of rope and went in search of one while I stayed to watch over my dog.

Jo sat on the narrow ledge howling intermittently, every now and then venturing to the cliff face as if seeking means of egress, but always returning to the same spot with a renewed burst of howling. I kept calling in case she could hear me but as she never looked up, I concluded that my voice couldn't reach her above the noise of the storm. I climbed down the rocks in my stockinged feet as far as possible to get closer to her and then called again, but still apparently in vain.

Time and again my eyes searched the face of the inlet seeking another way down, but it was hopeless without ropes.

I Remember My Training

SUDDENLY I realized I was sobbing and had been doing so for some time without it registering. I began to take myself to task. "What kind of occultist are you?" I asked myself. "What price now those years of training," while mentally recapping all I had learned.

Jo's howling had become softer—more of a whimper as if she was losing hope. Though I knew she couldn't hear me, I shouted down words of encouragement, telling her everything was going to be all right.

I was soaked to the skin, my feet were cut and bleeding, and yet from somewhere I gathered faith enough to feel hope and elation as I clung to the rocks and began to intone the God-names.

"Adonai ha-Aretz, Adonai Melekh, Adonai ha-Aretz, Adonai, Adonai, A-don-ai," I sang on and on, all the time watching the sea for the boat I *willed* to come.

Light was failing, the spectators had gone home, and the family was somewhere, trying in their various ways to get help. I was alone with the sea, the pitiless wind and rain and the occasional, desolate howling of JoJo. Still I kept on vibrating the God-names, invoking help for the dog below who had always been special to me. Sometimes I changed the ritual and called on Pan, promising, bullying, begging, "Sweet, sweet Pan."

Time Was Running Out

MY WATCH told me the family had been gone nearly two hours. Soon it would be dark and with it all hopes of rescuing Jo. I took up my intoning with fresh urgency, letting the God-names vibrate across the sea with all the strength and power of my being. I stopped visualizing a boat as I remembered that one did not tell the Gods what to do. Instead I visualized JoJo at the top of the cliff, well, happy and wagging her tail, and I held that mental picture as I called on the Gods unceasingly.

For some time I had been hearing what sounded like the echo of my own voice, and yet it wasn't my voice. I stopped intoning and listened. There it was, as clear as a repeating chorus: "Adonai haAretz, Adonai ha-Aretz."

The voices came from the sea, from the wind and from the air around. *The elements had taken up my song.* I clung perilously to the cliff, listening to that unearthly chanting. Looking down to the darkening sea, I could see faces forming in the white foam and hints of little figures as they bounced off the rocks and dived back into the seething waters. I don't know how long I stood there spellbound, looking and listening, but it is a memory forever engraved on my consciousness.

An Ordinary Man in Grey

THE SPELL was broken by a voice and I looked across the divide to the other side of the inlet where a man stood -- just an ordinary man in grey, nondescript clothing. He spoke, "Call her up now." I

ANGELS AND HEAVENLY VISITATIONS

obeyed unquestioningly and it never occurred to me not to, never giving a thought to the fact that JoJo couldn't hear me nor the impossibility of her making the ascent.

With a desperate urgency I shouted down to my dog, "JoJo! Jo, come along girl, there's a good dog, come on up." She lifted her head toward me, gave a single bark and bounded up the solid face of the rock. Realizing the danger of my own position on the cliff face right in the line of her ascent, I clambered as fast as I could to safe ground. Jo wasn't far behind me. She was strangely quiet and obviously suffering from shock as I hugged her to me.

The Family Returns

THEN everything happened at once. The family returned *en masse*: Ian with a coil of mucky rope, which he didn't think would be much help, and Mary and Andy to report on their unsuccessful attempt to get a fisherman to risk boat and life on an increasingly dangerous sea. Because of the poor light they didn't see Jo immediately, but when they did, they gaped with amazement and crowded around her expressing heart-felt relief, demanding, "But how? HOW?"

"A man told me to call her up," I explained inadequately.

"What man?" inquired my husband, peering through the mist.

I pointed across the horseshoe inlet and there was no man, nobody, just the swirling mist, the sea, the wind and the fast-gathering dusk.

Remembering that I hadn't thanked the Gods, I unashamedly threw up my arms to the rain and sky and cried out my gratitude while the family stared down at the sea below, and with a continuing mantra kept repeating it was impossible.

Impossible, yes. But it had happened. We discussed the miracle for most of the night. There was no way I could have heard a voice across the inlet, but I had. The cliff face inclined inwards and was impossible to scale but Jo had come up it, unaided. There could only be one answer . . . I had called upon the Gods and the Gods had answered. Was their emissary an angel in nondescript grey?

We rushed Jo some 20 miles to the vet. Apart from a few cuts and shock she appeared undamaged. Her toenails were the worst affected, frayed right down to the quick where she had struggled to heave herself from the water onto the rocks.

It wasn't until we arrived back at the hotel that we realized it was

September 29th, Michael's Day, named after the Archangel closest to humankind. Could the man have been Michael?

Editor's note: *In the Jewish (and magical) tradition there are many names for God. Adonai, Adonai Melech and Adonai ha-Aretz mean My Lord, My Lord and King and Lord of the Earth respectively. Pan is the Greek deity of the woods, fields and flocks.*

ANGEL—WITH WINGS!

Raye Wolfe
(Dec. 2000)

Do angels still have wings? They do as far as this Fate reader is concerned. She saw them with her own eyes—and so did another woman who was with her. They came during her friend's dark night of the soul.

THE FATHER of a good friend was dying of cancer. No one expected the old man to live through the night, so my friend asked me to stay with her as she sat vigil in the hospital.

Neither of us is particularly religious, although we both believe in angels and feel we are spiritual. However, as her father began to slip away shortly after midnight, my friend prayed aloud. She was frightened, and I longed to help her accept what was going to happen. I closed my eyes and said my own silent prayers to help this man go peacefully.

When I opened my eyes in the darkened room, I found myself squinting against flashes of light. As my eyes grew accustomed to the brightness, I watched vibrating lights surround the bed. They reminded me of wings fluttering. Each burst of energy shimmered and moved like the beating of dozens of tiny wings.

My friend didn't say anything at first, but she watched the lights, too. Later she told me she saw the fluttering out of the corner of her eye at first and was afraid to look directly at it because she was afraid that the light wasn't real. When we rather hesitantly asked each other what we were seeing, we felt relieved and awed to discover that we both saw the same thing.

The lights surrounded the bed for several minutes before disappearing. They left a serene peace, and my friend was able to calmly stay with her father as he died, a calmness neither of us felt before the lights appeared.

I believe that we saw the wings of angels that night, as they surrounded my friend's father and helped him, and us, prepare for his transition to the next world.

FRUGAL ANGELS?

Valenya
(May 2011)

Valenya is a longtime student of fringe sciences. In this essay she shares her findings about the manner in which heavenly presences most often answer our prayers for financial assistance.

Pennies from Heaven dropping in France?

LONG AGO, in what amounts to an earlier life, I hitchhiked around Europe with my then husband. Actually, we got very few rides especially in France. We spent a lot of time walking along the highway.

Although we'd brought several thousand in traveler's checks, we consistently changed too little money at a time and usually ran out of food and cash a long way from any town with a cooperative bank, though it didn't seem to matter.

In the afternoon, my husband would often declare that it was time for me to find some money, or we wouldn't eat that night. After he'd given me this "ritual" observation, I'd start scanning the shoulder of the road ahead of us as we marched, and almost always find something. Always coins and usually scattered far apart. Like over several miles.

This worked in a big way several times. Big, meaning enough to cover a room and/or dinner in an *appencion* in the next town. Usually I found enough to buy a loaf of bread and some cheese.

Where did it come from? Are the French so rich they toss money out of their cars?

I only found money while walking. Usually it was in small piles, but several times in a neatly stacked column of change.

Once, when I was 12, I was walking down the train tracks wishing I had 15 cents. That amount, plus what I'd already saved ($1.35), would buy me an hour's horse ride at the stables down the road. Several minutes later and less than 100 feet down the track I discovered three nickels sitting in a neat stack on a cross tie. Directly in front of me.

No, I wasn't mumbling and there was no one to hear me even if I had been. The open lots to each side were bare.

Another question. Were the coins there before I'd wished they were?

I never found bills, only coins. And once I started earning a regular income, I stopped finding them.

Has anything like this ever happened to you? Almost everyone I've told this story to had one of their own to offer in return.

They also often found just enough and not a penny more.

More Frugal Ghosts

IF YOU'VE READ the works of Robert Monroe you probably remember his "money pocket." One coat in his closet always had a small gift waiting for him. Usually only a few bills, but always welcome. Monroe tried covering the coat and sealing it in various ways, but the money kept coming.

The first time he was led to a cache, he was about 15. He was anticipating a school dance that he badly wanted to attend. But he needed about two dollars to go and couldn't figure out how to rustle it up.

The morning of the dance, he awoke with the conviction that if he was to lift an old board laying near the house, he would find the money underneath. That board had been lying there forever. Why would anyone put money under it? At first he tried to ignore the ridiculous idea, but after breakfast he gave in.

The plank was covered with dirt and leaves. It obviously hadn't been disturbed for a very long time.

Underneath it, he found wet dirt, a very startled colony of ants, and exactly two crisp, folded dollar bills. Not a penny more then he needed.

Buried Crosses and Bags of Coins

I JUST FINISHED reading *The Mystery of the Buried Crosses* by Hamlin Garland (for the second time).Written in the mid-'30s, most of the treasure it describes was discovered during the 1910s by an elderly, illiterate psychic lady, Mrs. Violet Parent, living in Redlands, California, who had an amazing gift for finding jewelry, crosses, gold and silver coins, and antique paper currency.

Through her guides, the spirits of Spanish Padres and Native Americans, Mrs. Parent directed her friends (and their healthy teenage sons) to dig up various caches of native treasures, hidden all over Southern and Central

California. She collected some 1,500 metal crosses. These were supposedly acquired through Arabian sea traders in the 1000s, Malian (West African) Traders during the 1300s, migrating Aztecs of the 1600s, and Southern California Indians as well as Spanish mission crosses, and early road markers in cruciform shape.

Not all of Mrs. Parent's findings were historical. She also found modern currency waiting for her on the road. Sometimes in parks, tied in cloth handkerchiefs, or in purses. She found a ten-dollar gold piece over the doorsill of her home. Once, she found loose bills in a bag of flour, another time, in a box of detergent. A stranger walked up to her in town and simply handed her a ten dollar bill, just as her Indian guide had predicted. Her husband, a clerk by occupation, dutifully recorded all these accounts in a ledger, which was provided at the end of Garland's book. Although the Parents were poor, they used only the money, saving all the crosses and giving the jewelry away as her guides directed.

When I told my partner Terry about this book, he asked me why the spirits never directed Mrs. Parent to a gold mine. Why not set her up for life, rather than dribble small bills in front of her? In fact, they once tried to lead her to a silver mine, but failed utterly.

John's "China Reeds"

SO AGAIN—why couldn't they find the mines? Because it would tempt them into greed? Terry puzzled over this. He doubted that was the reason, and of all people he should know.

The fact is, he once lived with an old miner who dowsed for gold over a map. John wasn't a greedy man, he only mined for as much as he needed. He subsisted mostly off avocados and day old bread, and lived in a small stone house on his ten acres, located at the edge of the desert east of Los Angeles.

Terry had just left home and was about 17, broke and currently without residence, when John invited Terry to move rent free into one of the outbuildings he'd constructed. Terry did just that (first chasing out the chickens) and learned to work silver in that shack, taking his first step toward become a working jeweler.

John was a wrestler in his youth and a Christian of a somewhat Gnostic cast. Later in his life he began to mine hard rock for gold, out in Nevada. But repeated (and unwarned) exposures to nuclear testing had given him a terminal case of cancer. Hard rock mining takes a team of healthy men. So he moved to the San Bernardino area and dowsed a map for gold instead.

He would unroll the map over the kitchen table. Then he'd take out a dowsing tool which he called a "China reed." And he'd dowse the map. Then he'd leave for a few days to go get his gold.

Sometimes a police car would come rolling down the drive toward the stone house. When John saw them coming he would fetch his China reed. And Terry would leave, if he happened to be visiting. It was just too creepy for him.

John would dowse for the person the police were seeking. Usually a body, by the time they'd given up and escorted to calling him. He could tell them if the person was still alive or dead. He must have been pretty good, considering how often they swung by.

The first time he'd done this, it was to find one of his own relatives. No one could find the body, so he'd offered to try. After that, he just helped whenever the police asked him. He felt that the gift of dowsing should be shared and never asked for money for his work.

A Tale of Two Batteries

LONG AGO, when Terry was young and always broke, he made a journey with friends, traveling from Southern California to Arizona. After eating at a truck stop on the state line, he returned to the car to resume the trip, but on turning the key got no response. Nothing mysterious there; the battery was dead. He'd had no money to replace it so had chosen denial as a strategy. And now they were stuck.

What to do? The three of them began to search and scan the shoulder of the road, away from the truck stop. Better than doing nothing. Almost immediately Terry noticed what appeared to be a battery hidden in the brush. "Nah," he thought. "It couldn't be any good!" After all, who chucks a good battery?

But it wasn't like he had any choice but to give it a try. There was a piece of wire lying next to it, so they tested it and got a powerful spark. Fully charged! And down the road they went.

But how did it come to be there, just waiting for him?

When Terry told my nephew Evan his battery story, Evan countered with one of his own.

More recently, Evan found himself in essentially the same situation. His battery was dead and he was broke.

He and some buddies had just spent a frozen night in Lake Tahoe, during one of the coldest nights ever recorded for that town. That night the thermometer plummeted to minus 15 degrees.

When they awoke in the morning, they found snow on the ground and the car's battery dead, the casualty of age and freezing.

The car was parked by itself, at the end of a lot, far away from any other vehicles. Here, Evan continues the story, in his own words:

"Right after trying to start the car for a few minutes, we popped the hood and looked in. I was standing just in front of the driver door, looking under the hood, and right when I said 'Dammit, this is going to be a hundred bucks!' I looked down at my feet, kind of as an admission of defeat. And a hundred-dollar bill was lying in the snow where my last footstep had been. If I hadn't gotten out and pushed the snow with my foot by accident it wouldn't have been possible to see it.

"We ended up walking two miles across South Lake Tahoe with the dead battery, because we had to exchange it in order to get the new one. After exchanging the old battery, the new one came to $99.96. It couldn't have been much closer to $100."

I should mention that Evan has also found money in other situations of intense need. Not much but enough. But why did he get the money and Terry get the battery when batteries were what both of them actually needed?

Worthwhile Beneficiaries?

MRS. PARENT spent her free days uncovering hidden history for the sake of Native American Spirits.

John the Miner helped people find missing relatives and the police find bodies, for free.

Robert Monroe wrote three books on astral travel, drawn from his own experiences, and then founded a center dedicated to teaching the art.

Did the Spirits simply consider them a good investment?

Of course this doesn't explain those batteries.

Or why some spirit left 15 cents on that railroad tie when I was 12 years old, or just enough cash for a hot meal while hitchhiking through France. I certainly didn't do anything to deserve either of those. Maybe sometimes, they just like to remind us we have more friends than we know?

THE "MONEY ANGEL" WHO MANIFESTED JUST ENOUGH

Ellen Marie Blend
(March 2013)

Apparently angels aren't there to answer our financial prayers by making us rich. Their job is simply to make sure we have enough to answer our actual needs. The rest, we are supposed to provide for ourselves. At least, that is the way this reader's "Money Angel" always responded.

I SEE visual imagery all of the time, but nobody talks to me. At least it is quite rare if they do. I'm expected to interpret the symbolic image that I see in order to get the message. I've often complained to the spirit world that I want to hear words.

Then one day while looking for information on the internet, I came across an article that explained how to clear your ear chakras so that you can hear your angels. So, when I went to bed, in my mind I fervently cleaned and scrubbed as directed.

I've known that I've had a "Money Angel" all of my life, as she has always made sure that I had just enough money. Sometimes a check would come in the mail, just when it was needed, or I would find small change on the ground, generally pennies, just to let me know that she was there. I've learned to count on her presence.

The first night an angel spoke to me, it was my "Money Angel," a female voice, who clearly said, "Here's a little money for you." I was in awe, but so pleased that she actually talked to me.

No one spoke to me again. So, I repeated the exercise of clearing the ear chakras. When I completed the cleansing, the next voice I heard was male, and he said, "You have nothing to fear."

WARNED BY AN ANGEL

Catherine Ponder

(Oct. 1964)

The words the "Angel of Death" awaken fear and dread in everyone who hears them. But perhaps we need to revise this view in light of the following reader's story. Perhaps this angel has another side and mission we have never imagined.

PERHAPS you have heard of the "angel of death," as I had many times. But little did I realize there really *is* an angel of death. My own recent experiences have convinced me that this angel is a celestial friend. I believe this angel ministers to both those who are taken and those who are left behind, during the transition experience commonly referred to as "death."

My husband and I had married just as I was completing my first book, *The Dynamic Laws of Prosperity,* two and one-half years ago. Our marriage was such a happy one, filled with many common interests, including my ministry and writing, and his career as a college professor.

Then one night in the fall of 1963, I awakened suddenly from a dream. No, it was more than a dream. It was a visitation—the kind the people of the Bible sometimes experienced.

An angel appeared at the foot of my bed in the middle of the night, waking me with the flapping of *his* wings. I intuitively knew he was the angel of death.

As this realization came over me, a cold feeling began in my heart and rushed swiftly upward through my throat and right out the top of my head. I sat upright in bed, instinctively placing my hands on my sleeping husband and crying out, "Oh no!" The angel disappeared.

This experience was so vivid that I did not sleep again that night. In the wee hours of the morning I prayed for guidance. Somehow I did not seriously believe this experience literally affected my husband. He always had been in good health and seemed destined for a long life and a distinguished scholastic career.

The next morning when I mentioned the episode to my husband, he placed little importance upon it. Instead, he put his arms around me protectively and said, "Honey, I don't want you having such strange experiences."

Three week later I knew what it meant.

One moment, my husband, only 40, was standing happily chatting with some of his students on the campus at the University of Texas where he taught. The next moment he was gone—dead from a heart attack.

It was then I remembered the angel of death. I remembered the cold feeling which had begun in my heart and rushed quickly upward. I believe (and it comforts me to believe) this is just the way my husband's soul left his body—quickly, without pain, from the heart upward.

Perhaps there had been one other warning of what was to come. For weeks my husband had been saying, "I keep having a dream that bothers me. In that dream I am again with people I have not seen for a long time, greeting them. The only thing I don't like about this dream is that I am in it alone. You are not there with me."

During the first week after his death, it was my turn to have a dream over and over—a dream that seemed related to the one he had had. I could see my husband standing in the sunshine, still dressed in his casual collegiate clothes. There was a gulf between us, but he was looking at me with that happy expression I had seen so often when all was well with him. He was surrounded by a throng of happy people. I had the impression they had been awaiting his arrival and were now thrilled to have him with them. It seemed such a happy time for everyone. My husband's only concern in this dream was that I understand that all was well, that this was the way it was to be.

This recurring dream helped me to release him.

I remembered having written about death in my new book, *The Prosperity Secret of the Ages*. My husband had worked with me closely on this manuscript, having completed final editing of it only the week before he died.

Now I reread my own words on death:

"Of all the hard conditions man has to overcome in the business of living, rising above the loss of a loved one through death is among the greatest challenges of all. But it can be met victoriously, when you realize there is no death, only new experiences in eternal life, which come *when the soul of man is ready for them.*"

After writing this passage on death, I had asked my husband's opinion. He had suggested that I make some additions. Now that he was gone this paragraph seemed his personal message to me:

"As in all situations involving human relationships, it is necessary to loosen up emotionally, let go and let God work for good in His own way.

Someone has said that when you take the 'u' out of 'mourning', it becomes 'morning'—a new morning for your loved one in another phase of life, and a new morning for you in your present life experiences."

fantastic

My husband had added these words to my manuscript in his own handwriting: *"Grief must give way to the new dawn."*

What could be plainer? I must emotionally loose him, let his soul go on to new experiences, happy though we had been in our joint earth venture.

Several weeks after his death, as I was going through his various papers, I found a statement of his spiritual beliefs, which he had written some years earlier. Here was another message to me:

"I believe that life is a school. We live in and attend the great 'University of Life.' We are here to learn to express our divine nature. I believe that life has several classrooms on this and other planes. I believe that we ascend or 'graduate' into new spheres of study *as our soul unfolds.*"

Later, in a notebook piled with his philosophical and spiritual thoughts, I found these instructions—again in his own handwriting:

"Release your loved ones in the calm assurance that they cannot get outside Infinity. You will then find release yourself, and go free to be happy."

There is an ancient saying that when the soul of man passes through the experience of death, an angel touches him and directs him. It comforts me to believe this, especially since the angel appeared.

It also inspires me to believe this same angel, as a direct ambassador of the Divine, is now touching and directing me in my continuing earthly journey. Perhaps the angel directed me to the comforting words my husband wrote on death, transition, release.

When you face the loss of a loved one through death, I hope you will consider the possibility that an angel touched and directed your loved one into new phases of eternal life, for which his soul was ready. Perhaps it will inspire you to believe this same angel now touches and directs you in your earthly journey. In this way your grief can give way to a new dawn.

The Psalmist may have been speaking of those on both sides of life when he promised: "For he will give his angels charge over to thee, To keep thee in all thy ways." (Psalms 91:11 ASV)

AN ANGEL'S REASSURANCE

Charlie Crouch
(Dec. 1996)

From a member in good standing of the U.S. Marine Corps whose veracity cannot be doubted comes a story of a childhood encounter with an angel who offered support during a horrific series of events.

I SAW an angel once.

I was eight years old, living in Kellogg, Idaho, when a noise upstairs woke me. I crept up the stairs, peeked over the top step, and saw my stepfather screaming and throwing things, and hitting my mother. I watched him tower over her, ranting. I watched tears run down her red face as he threw frozen foods, knick-knacks, and anything he could reach. I kept watching, wishing I could do something.

I imagined myself running from my hiding place and screaming at the top of my little voice, "Leave her alone!" I pictured it over and over, trying to get up my nerve. Instead, I stood there, staring at them and crying, making no sound so as not to give away my hiding place. It wasn't the first time I'd cried. I'd had no idea that in the years to come it would be a regular occurrence.

After the screaming was over, surprisingly, no one was bleeding. I crept back to my bed. It was then, with blurry, tear-filled eyes, that I saw an angel. She came in through the door of my bedroom, but she was floating—her head touched the top of the door. She had long hair, and she wore a flowing pink gown.

I was either too young or too surprised to be scared. The room filled with a good feeling and suddenly I didn't feel like crying any longer. I wiped my eyes and sat up in bed. Then she spoke. It seemed as if the words were both spoken out loud and in my head. She said, "Don't worry. Everything's going to be all right." I tried to figure out if I'd heard anything at all. She turned, and her dress moved and her hair swayed as she left.

The warmth she brought with her stayed even after she had gone. It warmed the room and calmed my fear.

The state authorities examined my family and determined my stepfather, with a little counseling, would be a fine father. He returned to my house and I lost hope. I believed that one of us wouldn't survive his reign. The last few months he lived with us were the worst. He pulled a loaded .45 pistol on his younger brother, who also lived with us, and he threw a television at my mother. I thought about the angel a lot. I thought no hope was left except the angel. She was the one secret no one else knew. She was my one pleasure and kindness. Often, I prayed, even begged, for her to return.

It was four years before my stepfather left my house. Despite those years, I believe my angel was right.

Today, I have a great job in the Marine Corps. I have watched the sunset from 3,000 feet, flying alone in a Cessna above flooded Missouri farm fields. I have watched the moon set over the East China Sea. I have sat at the top of eight hundred feet of granite, exhausted and happy. I've met wonderful people from a multitude of countries, tasted strange foods, and danced with people from Japan and Nigeria.

And I wonder, would I have had the courage to take on such grand adventures if my angel hadn't assured me that my fear wouldn't last forever?

STAIRWAY TO HEAVEN: THE STORY OF THE ENTOMBED MINERS

Bill Schmeer

(March 1965)

Trapped underground for fourteen days and given up for dead, David Fellin and Henry Throne were never alone. Their companions were angels, who offered comfort and strength. Surely one of the most amazing stories ever to appear in the pages of FATE.

EARLY on August 3, 1963, three men turned their backs on the morning sun and disappeared into the blackness of an old, independently-operated coalmine at Sheppton, Pennsylvania. Fourteen days later two of the men would step back into the sunlight, bringing with them an astounding report of a continuous, collective hallucination which the editors of *Fate* assure me is unmatched in the annals of psychic research.

To give a name—"collective hallucination"—to the experiences David Fellin and Henry Throne shared in their accidental tomb 390 feet deep in the earth, is certainly not to explain the phenomena. This scientific description indicates that the two men simultaneously saw objects which in fact had no reality. But has science catalogued all aspects of reality?

I can only warn the reader that the two central figures in this report object vehemently to implications that they imagined any part of the story they are revealing in full detail for the first time on these pages.

Fate actually started to work on this story when Associated Press bulletins issued during the rescue operations hinted that the cave-in victims were experiencing unusual phenomena. Subsequent newspaper stories indicated that both survivors claimed their temporary tomb was illuminated by a strange light of unknown origin; that they had seen two men dressed like power company linemen; that they saw white marble stairs leading out of the mine; and that Pope John XXIII was present with them in the mine.

Little further detail was forthcoming on these reports and a *Fate* reporter sent to the scene found the survivors unable to talk to him because the Associated Press had bought exclusive "rights" to this news story.

However, after the first anniversary of the accident I was able to conduct independent interviews with both of the survivors. Neither man is yet aware that I have interviewed his companion and I doubt that they have spent any significant period of time together putting their views into agreement, since each has a rather wary attitude toward the other. So you, the reader, are really the first authority to study the degree of correspondence existing between the memories of these two survivors of one of the most terrifying experiences men have ever lived through.

The terrible saga of Dave Fellin and Hank Throne began near 9:00 o'clock on a Tuesday morning. The two men, along with co-worker Louis Bova, just had filled a rail car (called a mine buggy) with coal and had sent it up the nearly vertical shaft of the old mine. Fellin, 58, a veteran of 43 years of mining, was foreman and co-owner of the mine; Throne, 28, had been on the job only two months; Bova, 43, was a thoroughly experienced miner.

The buggy of coal was drawn to the mouth of the shaft by the winch operator, dumped and headed back down the hole. Halfway down the buggy stopped. The operator tried again. Again the car stopped. The winchman knew there had been a cave-in and he raced away for help.

At the bottom of the shaft, the cave-in had begun with a roar of splintering timber and the crash of falling rock. The three men working there jumped for their lives. Two to one side of the shaft, and one to the other.

Fellin and Throne were the two who jumped together to the same side of the shaft. They found themselves uninjured, but in cramped quarters. Taking stock of their survival equipment, they found that besides their own hands and legs, they had only their miner's lamps, a little water in a jug, a broken axe, a crowbar, an old saw and a rasp.

The men were near the 390-foot level of the mine, which, ironically, put Dave Fellin just a few hundred yards from his own house where his wife, Anna, waited for his return.

In addition to these scanty tools, the men did have the advantage of Dave Fellin's years of experience underground, his courageous attitude, and his fund of general knowledge.

Young Hank Throne, like Fellin a native of the immediate neighborhood, had his youth and strength to put into the battle for their lives. Hank had worked only five years in coal mines, but he earlier gained valuable experiences during an eight-year tour of duty in the army. Hank also had a wife waiting for him back on top.

Both men knew that essentially it was futile to try to dig out with the tools at hand, but the veteran Fellin was determined to try. Together they began to inch their way up the side of the debris-clogged shaft, hoping against hope that they would meet a rescue party working its way down from the top.

After wracking efforts, they fought their way to a gangway 30 to 40 feet above their starting point. This gangway was an old working area with no outlet, but there was room to move around, so the miners decided to rest until they could determine which way the activity was going on the surface.

Their morale might have been shattered had they known that the authorities planning their rescue were unable to mount any effort as long as rock and debris continued to plummet from the sides of the shaft to the bottom.

While waiting for some evidence of a rescue attempt, Fellin and Throne went on with their own attempts to reach the third miner, Lou Bova, trapped somewhere on the other side of the shaft. At one point Dave Fellin thought he heard Lou yell, "Come for me. I'm hit [or hurt]!"

Dave asked Lou to give the miner's rap, a signal of two long and three short raps. He asked for this signal because Bova contracted laryngitis easily. Fellin called several times, and he believes that Bova answered once with the miner's signal. But there were no further signals or calls and Bova's body never has been recovered.

Three days after the cave-in started, state and private mine experts decided that rescue of any survivors was impossible, and recommended the mine shaft be filled and a new shaft dug to recover the bodies. However, the families of all three miners were convinced their men were alive, and they prevented this drastic action, which would mean death to any living thing trapped in the old shaft.

Joe Fellin, Dave's brother, was more than just convinced that his brother survived; he claimed he "knew it" although he had been estranged from his brother. The men, though living close to one another, had not spoken in 20 years. Himself an old hand in the Pennsylvania anthracite fields, Joe believed that if a shaft could be drilled just beyond the main slope of the mine, the trapped men could be rescued.

Saturday, the fifth day following the cave-in, a giant drilling rig was assembled over the spot selected by Joe Fellin. It was put to work drilling a six-inch hole to a gangway, which Joe claimed existed 390 feet below.

Around midnight Saturday the desired depth was reached and the drill bit was withdrawn. One of the rescue workers leaned into the mouth of the bore hole and called down. To his great surprise he got an answer!

An engineer from a radio news mobile unit immediately stripped the hardware from all his microphone cables, spliced them together and dropped a mic down the hole. Dave Fellin then made his first contact with the outside world since Tuesday morning, five days before.

After drilling this first hole, which was used as a supply and communications line, workers made three heartbreaking attempts to drill a rescue shaft. One attempt missed the underground cavern, one attempt almost caved in the roof of the miner's refuge, and the third try finally succeeded. After 14 days underground, the men were eased to the surface, one at a time, in a parachute harness.

When they reached the top, the two were rushed to a hospital where Fellin requested a psychiatric examination—his experiences had caused him to fear the loss of his sanity—and where Throne received treatment for a hand injured striking something that skeptics claim he imagined.

Examination by two psychiatrists confirmed that both Fellin and Throne were mentally alert and competent. But no examination then or now can establish the reality, or non-reality, of the experiences that remain the most vivid memories held by the two principals in this dramatic event. Here, then, are the details of the entombment that hitherto have remained unspoken.

As a general description of the strange events 390 feet below the surface of the earth, Dave Fellin told me, "Pope John and the cross was there all the time. But these other things kept jumping across. They would come like a movie. First there was these men with lights and after a while the steps would come . . . . It was real. Both of us were seeing it and we knew they was live people. We know that."

Pope John first appeared to the men during their second 24 hours underground. The Pope and a gold cross appeared on the cavern wall behind Fellin, but Hank Throne was the first to mention the apparition. Throne, a Protestant, did not recognize the figure, and asked Fellin who it was. Fellin, a Roman Catholic, identified the figure but avoided looking at its face. Fellin had been aware of the presence, but had not spoken of it for fear that he was seeing things.

Both men volunteered to me that they had seen Pope John in their tomb. Hank Throne described the figure's face as smiling and happy. Dave Fellin never saw the face because he did not attempt to look. But by casting his glance downward he saw a foot and part of a leg.

Both men independently agreed that the Pope stayed with them until the successful escape shaft broke through to them. They also agreed that the shaft broke through at the exact spot where the figure of the Pope had been seen throughout their trials.

A gold cross became visible to the men at the same time they first saw the Pope. There is some variation in their descriptions of this appearance. Fellin saw it as smooth bands of gold metal. He described the members of the cross as being straight with squared ends, except that the left side of the transverse beam curved upward at its outer extremity.

Throne described the members of the cross as having rounded ends. He also described the transverse beam as curving down on the left side and up on the right side. The upper end of the vertical member, he said, curved slightly to the right above the intersection with the transverse.

After the Pope and the cross, ". . . there was these men with lights."

Dave Fellin told me that the men came in a chariot-like vehicle which had no horses to draw it. Only the top parts of their bodies could be seen and then only in profile. The men wore lights on their foreheads. The lights were in the shape of funnels, Dave said, with the narrow end of the funnel-shape emitting waves of light, as opposed to narrow beams.

Hank Throne said he first saw these men unreeling wire from a spool. He said they wore utility belts, miner's lamps with battery packs, and looked like "ordinary guys." It was Hank who labeled them "linemen." Hank asked them to bring light into the cavern and they responded by disappearing for about an hour.

But buried 390 feet in the earth, the men did have light. Dave Fellin recalls, "It was a bluish light. Sort of like steam. The whole room, the whole area was filled up with steam, and you could see shadows."

Fellin said the light would start from a point the size of a match head and would grow until it filled the room. It was soft light, he noted, but bright enough to read his watch by or to see to take care of Throne's injured hand. Fellin has asked skeptics to explain the amount of work he and Throne did, difficult work such as placing timbers to prop the ceiling of the mine shaft, if the only light they could see by was a product of their imaginations.

Fellin also added that when the light came, and it appeared to him only intermittently, it seemed to lift the men from their underground chamber to a place where they could see for miles.

Hank Throne's recollection was that the bluish light was there all the time, not just intermittently. Hank said the light was bright enough to read a watch by, and that it had no apparent source but filled the entire area.

Throughout their entire 14-day entrapment, the only event that either man admits was frightening was the sudden appearance of a set of white marble stairs that seemed to lead up and out of the rock-crowded mine shaft.

Dave Fellin said the stairs were white marble, ten to 12 feet wide, and straight and steep. He thought they went right up until they disappeared from sight.

Hank Throne described the stairs as white marble, but he thought they were "three to four people wide." He also recalled them as being 12 to 14 in number, and narrowing toward the top.

Hank wanted to climb the stairs, but Dave Fellin objected. Dave was afraid that if they went up the steps it would be the end of them. Specifically, Dave thought the steps led to Heaven. The men's recollections are in absolute agreement on this exchange.

Although the men were trapped for more than five-and-a-half days before there was any real reason to expect rescue, this was the only incident that made them fearful. They are in agreement that one reason for the absence of fear during the ordeal was that three men had come to them with a tablet or plaque which showed they would survive.

In describing this incident, Dave Fellin said, "I don't remember what day it was. I was just thinking, 'Is any of us going to get out?' And the minute I thought that, why the three men came, one with the plaque."

Fellin described these men as ruggedly handsome, about six feet three inches tall, with bronze-colored skins and very slightly pointed ears. He said they had thin lips and "normal" eyes and that their physical condition reminded him of football players. The only costume he described was a wide head band, open on top to reveal dark, straight hair.

Dave described the plaque as being orange in color, about eight by 11 inches on the face and three-fourths of an inch thick.

Hank Throne described the three visitors as having high cheek bones, Caucasian eyes, and thin lips. He said their skin was darker on the hands and toes than on the faces. Their hair, he said, was ear-length, combed back at the top and left to fall at the sides. He said they wore nothing on their heads, but were robed in green-gray garments similar to Japanese kimonos and wore open sandals of their feet.

The plaque, Hank recalled, was triangular, almost heart-shaped. He estimated its dimensions as about 16 inches long and 24 inches wide. Its color was blue, and it was covered with rows of holes with pegs about the size of a cigarette filling most of the holes.

One row of holes was open and one of the three visitors asked Dave Fellin to put a peg in a hole. As Dave plugged in his peg the board got darker. Hank refused to place a peg when he was asked.

Fellin told me there were names on the plaque and that he tried to see if his and Throne's names were included. But when the visitors agreed to show the plaque to Fellin, ". . . there was nobody's name on there. It was empty. So I knew me and Hank was gonna come out." Having thus reassured Dave and Hank, the three visitors vanished.

Both men later saw other groups of mysterious people in idyllic scenes—people who seemed to glow with an aura of beauty. During one episode Dave and Hank report having had the feeling of walking through the scene until they reached the white marble stairs they had seen before. They saw people going up the stairs to a set of double doors closed across the top of the steps.

Some of those who went up the stairs were admitted through the doors; others were not. Hank Throne wanted to go up the steps, but Dave told him not to go. Hank asked for a tool. He was going to break down the doors. As Hank hammered at the doors the scene suddenly disappeared and Hank hit the wall of the mine shaft, injuring his hand. Everything then went dark in the shaft for 30 minutes to an hour.

This was the last major event before the drill first broke through to the men. However, as soon as the communications hole was established a new sight was seen by both men: small, childlike creatures that danced around the communications shaft each time that food was sent down by the rescue party.

Both men agree that these figures could be seen even in the full light of flashlights furnished by the rescue team. Although some writers have described these figures as angels, neither man used that word in our interviews.

Both men also agree that on another occasion a figure both identify as an American Indian chief stood in the communications shaft for several hours.

These were the only phenomena experienced during the first three days after contact was re-established with the outside world. Except, of course, for the figure of Pope John which remained visible to the men until the final moments of rescue.

However, three days after the communications shaft came through, the men witnessed a scene in which the figures appeared ugly and grotesque, rather than happy and contented as they had been in every previous instance.

All of the details of this scene are from the interviews with Dave Fellin. Hank Throne did not volunteer any information on this specific episode.

Fellin recounted to me a scene in which he and Throne saw people walking toward them in pairs—sometimes two men, sometimes two women, sometimes a man and a woman.

As the figures approached they became altered and grotesque. Faces became distorted, arms and legs dropped away.

From this confrontation, Fellin turned aside and walked, or believes he walked, into another scene where he saw a beautiful garden. The people in this scene looked like ordinary mortals, he said, but beauty seemed to flow from their bodies.

All the figures Dave saw in this scene were adults; there were no children. Figures moved into the scene and took seats at tables in groups of three and four. Some of the figures would pause on entering the scene to look toward the two trapped men, "like they were judging," Dave remembered.

The garden stretched as far as Dave's eye could see; in fact he thought he could see as far as California. Dave said that he felt as though he could leave his body and look back to see himself sitting on the mine floor.

Fellin recognized the faces of at least 12 people in this scene. Some were friends no longer living, but others were still alive when I interviewed Dave. Dave made no effort to communicate with any of these figures.

This was the final event before rescue. After hospitalization and after medical authorities had assured themselves that both men were sound in body and mind, Dave Fellin and Hank Throne picked up the threads of their lives.

Hank Throne went back to mining for a brief time after the accident, but now works on a bridge-building project on the Interstate Highway System, near Hazleton, Pennsylvania. Hank continues to be a regular church attendant, but he has not become more or less religious.

Dave Fellin also went back into the mines after the accident, but his job ran out and for the first time in his life he is now working outside the mines, driving a school bus. Dave, too, remains only an ordinary church-goer.

Fellin and Throne merged from their joint tomb victorious over incredible mental and physical punishment. But the cruelest blow was yet to be struck—the blow aimed at their integrity by lesser men who could not believe.

The frustration this breeds is evident in Dave Fellin who insisted on a psychiatric examination after the rescue and who has offered, in my presence, to be tested or examined by anyone who doesn't believe him. And I will be swift to testify that Dave's offer is as sincere as his belief that every detail he put into the report you have just read is a true and accurate statement of fact.

PART IV

GUARDIAN ANGELS

*A*CCORDING to one widespread belief, every person has an angel appointed to watch over them from the moment they are born till the moment of their death. This angel's job is to guide that person, protect them from harm, and prompt them to choose the right path at times of great temptation. In this section you will learn from those who are in touch with their own, how to become attuned to your guardian angel, learn its name, recognize its promptings, and contact it directly when you are in need of advice.

YOU HAVE A GUARDIAN ANGEL

G. H. Irwin
(Raymond A. Palmer)
(May 1949)

Do guardian angels really exist and attempt to counsel and aide us throughout our lives? Here Fate Magazine founder Raymond A. Palmer (who edited Fate under the name Robert N. Webster), writing under another of his many pseudonyms, gives his own personal answer.

THE WATER is deep and treacherous, the current swift, the overhanging bank crumbling . . . and the small boy sits there happily fishing, in grim danger of his life!

Suddenly he starts guiltily. Into his mind's eye flashes a vision of his mother's stern face, his father's beckoning finger, the woodshed. . .

"Gosh, gee, I'd better be gettin' home, or Paw will tan the hide offa me!"

Hastily he winds up his fishing line, scrambles to his feet, sets off for home. Behind him there is a splash, and the bank on which he had been sitting collapses into the water, which swirls muddily, angrily, for a moment, as though cheated of its prey. But the little boy is oblivious of his narrow escape, nor is there any eye to see the death that might have been his.

Or is there?

All through the ages mankind has believed in guardian angels. There are millions of persons living today who would be positive that it was something more than the voice of "conscience" which spoke to the little boy and started him from his dangerous position on the precarious riverbank. These millions would say that his guardian angel had been watching over him,, had contacted his mind in some mysterious, soundless way, and sent him scurrying off to safety.

There are millions more who would scoff.

"Chance," they would say. "Mere chance," "The oddity known as coincidence," or "It just happened that way."

But what is the truth of the matter—if the truth *can* be determined at all? And lacking positive proof, what is the evidence for, or against, the existence of a guardian power beyond the ability of our normal, everyday senses to detect?

During the past 20 years, this writer has investigated many strange things, gone into his investigations with what he likes to call "the scientific method". The scientific method is to experiment, interview, observe . . . and fit the observable facts with a hypothesis, which will fit the greatest number of them. That is science's way of determining truth, as closely as it can be determined. The theory which fits the greatest known number of conditions definitely proven to exist, is the *most* truthful answer to the problem of the truth of the matter. What, then, can we say, definitely, about guardian angels, or protecting forces which watch over us?

First, there are the writer's personal experiences, several of which he will list here. The first instance occurred some 15 years ago. The writer was sitting in his own living room, located at the other end of the house from the rear porch, which was a second-story affair with a wooden railing around it. Below was a concrete-paved back yard. Suddenly, inexplicably, while reading the newspaper, this writer leaped to his feet, dashed madly through the house, and out onto the back porch—just in time to grasp his two-year-old brother by the arm and lift him back over the railing to safety. The youngster's hold had slipped, and he was just beginning a plunge that would have resulted in certain injury, if not death.

Another incident involving a youngster occurred more recently, while the writer was driving home from his office. A half-block from a parked car, the strange feeling that a child was about to dart out into the path of the writer's car from behind that parked vehicle, caused the writer to slow down almost to a crawl. At precisely the time the car would have reached the parked one had it continued its speed, a small child, invisible behind it, lurched into the street. There would have been no chance to avoid striking him, had the writer not been forewarned.

The final incident was considerably more dramatic to your writer, since it concerned his own safety and narrow escape from death. It happened during a fishing trip. Arriving before dawn, the party found it impossibly dark and decided to wait for the approaching daylight before taking off in the boats. Your writer decided to kill time by climbing a hill beside the river and, arriving at the top, watching for the first faint advent of the sunlight. At the top the horizon was dimly visible, and intervening, what seemed to be a level, flat plain. Yet he stood stock still, sensing something wrong. The ground seemed to give a little just at the toes. Turning, the writer climbed back down to where the party waited, not staying to see the beauty he had come to observe. Dawn came, and curiosity became uppermost. Once more climbing the hill, the brink of a precipice some 80 feet high was revealed. There in the soft earth at the edge was the imprint of a shoe-toe. One step more. . .

Curious as to these unexplainable cases of "foreknowledge" of disaster, the writer asked hundreds of people about their own experiences, or lack of them, of a similar nature. It can safely be said that almost everyone will admit to at least one outstanding instance.

Most interesting experiences came from parents of very small children. Said one man: "Guardian angels? Most certainly! I and my children's guardian angels are on the best of speaking terms !"

And he actually meant "speaking" terms. . .

"Take the other night," he told me. "I was wakened out of a sound sleep by a voice—which I swear was still echoing in the room as I leaped out of bed. It just said three words: 'Dan! The baby!' and I made tracks into the baby's room. Smothering, that's what she was! It was a narrow escape."

He went on to tell me that night after night he would obey the promptings of the invisible voice, and he swore that never did the voice (sometimes audible, but mostly not) mislead him. Always there was a necessity for his presence in either one of the children's rooms. Perhaps they had kicked off the bedclothes and were becoming chilled; or the younger one had wet the bed and required a change; or a leg or arm become twisted in the slats of the bed.

"And, you know," he confided, "It's a woman's voice. She must be a whiz—completely competent, and on the job every minute! I feel sort of safe about those kids of mine. . ."

Said another man: "You asking me questions like that makes me think of a theory I've had about my clock. You see, I usually set it for 6:45 every morning, and just about two seconds before it rings, I wake up and reach out to turn it off. Happens every morning. I haven't wound that alarm in a year! Habit, I used to think. Then I noticed that one morning after I'd set the clock for a half-hour earlier, I beat the bell to the punch by the same two seconds. I figured maybe the clock's works made some little noise just before it rang, which woke me up, so I checked on that, but if it makes a noise, I can't detect it while awake. So, I kinda like to think it's my own guardian angel, waking me up at the right time every morning, and saying 'Joe, shut off the alarm before you wake up the whole family.'"

The subconscious mind, says one school of thought. But if that theory is correct, it gives an amazing array of powers to the subconscious! The power to see the future; the power to see at a distance; the power to see in the dark; the power to form habits instantaneously; the power to receive thought waves; and many other inexplicable abilities equally hard to rationalize.

To the student of the world's religions, the idea of a guardian angel is well established. All religions postulate the existence of these mysterious watchers in one way or another. Some even describe groups of angels working in shifts, as many as ten to a person, or one to ten persons. Especially are children supposed to have constant attendants, adults sometimes losing the protection, a penalty for disregard.

Not only is the guardian angel entrusted with the protection from harm of its charge, but with a myriad of other duties. It acts as the voice of conscience, directing, correcting, suggesting. It teaches, instructs, implants. It wards off evil influences. It battles mightily with demons and the devil himself. It comforts, calms, heals.

Even among savage races, members of no organized religion, the concept of a guardian spirit is strong and sure. In the case of the atheist, the belief in "hunches", in "chance", in "luck" is quite marked.

And strangest of all, the absolute unbeliever has a complex rationalization in which he has built up such ideas as the subconscious, the mass mind, a sixth sense, cause and effect, predetermination by the normal course of events.

Says he: "The inevitable result of a series of experiences is to build up a predictable reaction to a repetition of the opening events of a chain of events leading up to a conclusion. It is by this method, the recognition of a *pattern of occurrence* through past experience, that one predicts the appearance of a child from behind a parked car. Once before, the observer saw a similar occurrence, and the experience became a part of his subconscious reflex."

Yes, it could all be explained that way, but. . .

The other day the writer talked to a man who told an incredible story.

"I've got a three-year-old daughter," he said. "One day I saw her do something I can't explain. She had been sitting, quietly playing with her dolly, when she suddenly climbed to her feet, toddled over to where her five-year-old brother was playing beneath a tree. 'Dickie don't want head hurt,' she said solemnly, and dragged him insistently with her toward the middle of the yard—just before a large branch, loosened by a storm of a few days previous, fell precisely where Dick had been playing."

"Perhaps she saw the loosened branch beginning to sag," the writer suggested.

"No," he said, "I asked her that, and I just couldn't make her understand. All she would say was: 'God didn't want me to let Dickie get hurt on the head.'"

A subconscious reflex conditioned by experience? Perhaps, but *whose?*

Your writer believes in guardian angels, and he doesn't care who knows it!

GUARDIAN ANGELS WATCH OVER ME—AND YOU!

W. H. Ziegler

(Sept. 1967)

One World War II vet recounts here how various members of his family were protected by guardian angels over three generations.

IN AUGUST 1945, while serving in the armed forces on Iwo Jima, I had my first experience with the "unknown." We had landed on the island under heavy fire, into the middle kettle of hell you might say. Our command was to dig in fast and we didn't need any urging. I dug like crazy, then dove into what little protection I had. I heard the screams of one of our men who had stepped on a mine; the whole lower part of his legs was blown off. Man, at a time like that you really pray!

Things kept getting worse out there and I thought it was the end of the line for us all. Then suddenly someone was there in the hole with me, someone had come to protect me. This invisible guardian angel stayed with me all through that long and terrible night. Once, when things were quiet out there for a minute, I decided to look out but an unseen force shoved me down just as a bullet whizzed by my face.

A few years later when I home again and while I was on vacation I spent a long, long afternoon with my grandmother. This good woman was more a mother to me, for she raised me. My mother died when I was five and the only thing for my three-year-old little sister and me to do was live with Grandma. I thank God for the kind of woman she was, kind and good to us.

Now as we talked Grandma said, "Jim, I have a note I'd like to give you. I found it on the desk upstairs a few days after your mother passed away. Your mother must have had a premonition that she was going to die."

She handed me a slip of paper that was yellow with age. Mother simply stated that she felt her time here was short, wanted Grandma to raise us, and even though her frail body was separated from us, her spirit would stay close to guide and protect us.

"When little Ann was nine she almost died from a ruptured appendix. Your mother stood at the head of Ann's bed all through one bad night," Grandma said. "She didn't leave until we knew Ann was out of danger. I've

122

felt the presence of her spirit many times."

Grandma sat rocking there on the porch with a faraway look in her eyes, then she said, "Once I had a very real and disturbing experience with the unknown. Pa and I were living on a ranch out in Wyoming about 1910. I had four children desperately ill; I was seven months pregnant, then all at once in the middle of the night my child was born dead. Doctors were so few in that area; the nearest one was at Afton, twenty miles away. There were no telephones anywhere near. I had a high fever: peritonitis had set in and I was dehydrating. Pa knew he should get a doctor fast. It was spring, we had two feet of snow and he would have to put on snowshoes. But the hardest part of it all, he would have to leave me alone while he went. After banking the fire and making me as comfortable as possible, he leaned over to kiss me good-bye. Tears were streaming his face as he asked God to protect and give me strength while he was away.

"I must have gone to sleep and when I woke up," —here she paused and looked me in the eye. "Jim," she said, "I'm sure I was awake! There was an old man sitting by my bed. He had long white hair and the kindest, most beautiful face I have ever seen. He had on sort of a loose robe and his feet were bare. I felt no fear, just a wonderful feeling of relief that I was no longer alone. He got up, came over and put his hands on my head. He told me I must have courage, my life would be spared and I would bear other children. The most wonderful feeling came over me. My body felt warm and weightless, the dreadful pain left and I drifted off to sleep. It didn't seem like any time at all until Pa and Doctor Proctor were in the room.

"The first thing Pa said was, 'Mary, has someone been here?'

"'Yes,' I said, 'a kind old man came and sat at the side of my bed while you were gone.'

"Pa just wiped his eyes and couldn't say a word but the doctor told me they had seen an old man going down the dry creek bed as they came through the field. The thing that puzzled them was there were no tracks in the snow anywhere."

In the fall of 1959 we got word to come home at once; Grandma was not expected to live. She was past eighty and quite feeble but her mind was exceptionally sharp and active.

Her youngest son, Fred, had been killed in a car accident that June. The decision of the family had been not to tell her about this tragedy. Fred had been faraway for a long time and there really was nothing she could do about his death but grieve. So she wasn't told of his death. Then soon after, like a bolt from the blue, Aunt Louise died of a heart attack. Again the family decided they just would not tell Grandma about her daughter's death. Consequently Grandma did not know about either Fred's or Louise's death.

While my wife and I sat at her bedside during her final hours she rambled some, talking in delirium. She was in her own room at home. Grandpa had died in this same room nine years before.

Suddenly Grandma sat straight up in bed, her eyes bright. She looked at me and said, "Jim, get my dress quick; Pa is corning to take me with him. Hurry, Jim, hurry."

I just took her frail old hand in mine and said, "Yes, Grandma." Then she leaned forward peering out the window. The curtain was blowing in the soft autumn breeze. "He's here," she said. "Father is here."

I looked out the window but of course I saw no one. Nevertheless, I felt my scalp tighten as she said, "Bless my soul, Fred and Louise are with him and there's Mary Ann!" (Mary Ann was my mother.)

A few minutes later the doctor signed the death certificate. I stood looking down at her. She wore a half-smile and a look of utter content on her face. Somehow since then I don't dread death as I used to.

There have been other times when I've felt the power of the unknown. An incident that happened a few months ago prompted me to write this article.

Our children have a small electric heater upstairs. They use it during the summer while the gas furnace is off, because sometimes our nights get pretty cold. I usually check this heater the last thing before I go to bed just to make sure all is well. But on this particular night I was dog-tired and I had no idea the kids would turn the heater on anyway, because we were having a warm spell. In the middle of the night Grandma called me. Her voice was loud and clear and I recognized it immediately. "Check upstairs! Your children are in danger," she called. I leaped out of bed and ran upstairs. The heater was on full blast, and Ted had left his clothes so close to it they were scorching. I pulled the plug, removed the scorched clothes and went to bed. My wife asked sleepily, Is something wrong?"

"Hell," I said, "if Grandma hadn't called me, we might all have burned up."

She raised up on an elbow, looked at me sort of funny and asked, "Grandma called you?"

Not till she repeated this question did I realize Grandma doesn't live here anymore. But she did call me!

HOW TO SEE YOUR GUARDIAN ANGEL AND BECOME ATTUNED TO ITS ADVICE

Dawn C. Athay
(Dec. 1996)

Doubters often ask, "If guardian angels are all around us, how come I never see mine or hear the advice it gives?" Dawn C. Athay says anyone can learn to see and hear their guardian angel, and tells us how.

I HAVE ALWAYS believed in guardian angels. After my son was born two years ago, I felt a newfound interest in spirituality, and I began trying to communicate with my guardian angel. I tried prayer, and even a Ouija board, all to no avail. Then I learned about Erica Chopich.

Chopich, a Los Angeles-based counselor, can see, hear, and talk to angels wherever she goes. With just a little practice, her methods can work for anyone who wants to contact the benevolent spirits that guide and protect all of us.

Chopich has seen angels since she was a child. She was taught, however, that her gift was shameful—so she blocked the angels out for 3.5 years. One day, however, her angel appeared to her and told her she must use her ability to help other people. At first she refused. As a doctor of psychology, she said, "I didn't want anybody to think I was nuts." But the angels were relentless. She saw them in shopping malls. She saw them in her sleep. She saw them everywhere. Finally she agreed to do readings for people.

Chopich explained that angels, or "master teachers," as she calls them, are really white light or colored energy. They often take human form, however, so that we can identify with them.

Everyone has a guardian angel who watches over them exclusively, Chopich said. There may be other spirits around us at times, checking on us or helping us, but our guardian angels never leave our side.

Chopich told me quite a bit about angels: Their love for us is divine, so pure that it's hard for us humans to understand, she said. We are the most important thing to them. We could never make them angry. We could never disappoint them. They never judge us. They just love us and try to steer us to the best path.

Every day of our lives, our angels try to put us in situations that will help us. They may put somebody to meet in our path. They might try to steer us to the right books or television shows. They even try to protect us from dangerous people and dangerous circumstances.

Our angels know us inside and out. They know our every thought, and they know what problems we have. They help us with family or work, and sometimes they delight us with good news to come. They are wise, and they have an answer for every question.

Sometimes, however, they won't answer our questions. That's because we are all students, here on this Earth to learn. Dealing with tough situations helps us grow—and growth is sometimes painful. Sometimes our angels will even test us to see if we have learned from experience.

Our Angels Protect Us

WHEN I first met Chopich, she saw my angel right away, She described him to me: His name is "Michael," and he is very striking to look at. She said he is tall, thin, and powerful looking, with twinkling blue eyes and a quick smile, and full, dark, shoulder-length hair, with just enough grey to make him look very distinguished. He looks about 50 years old, she said.

I couldn't hear or see Michael. But Chopich did. She asked me if my right side was warmer than my left, because Michael was hovering there and stroking my hair. I was disappointed that I could not feel his presence, but she told me that in the future I would be able to, if I began working with him.

Michael was thrilled at the chance to talk with us. In fact, when she first made contact with him, Chopich had to tell him to slow down. Most angels, she said, are so happy to talk to her that they give her more information than she can take in at once.

Michael described some of the ways he had protected me during my lifetime. In return, I told Michael that once, when I tripped and broke my leg, it felt like somebody had pushed me. Michael admitted that he had pushed me, but he said that his push actually kept me from dislocating my hip, which would have been far more serious. I was thrilled to think that I had actually felt my guardian angel.

My husband, a construction worker, also had a reading with Chopich.

He asked if his angel, named Daniel, had ever saved him from harm. Daniel laughed and said that he had saved him many, many times, especially at work.

Daniel said, "Remember that day at work when you dropped a tool, but nobody got hurt? That was me." My husband vividly remembered that day. He had dropped a heavy tool from a high ladder and he had jumped down to see if anyone was hurt, apologizing profusely because the tool could have killed anyone it had struck.

Daniel also described the day my husband and I installed new tiles on our roof. It had just started to rain when I looked up and saw my husband slip. I couldn't grab him—I could only scream as he slid down the roof. Just before he plunged off the edge, his fall stopped. There was nothing to stop him. He just stopped. The angel, Daniel, said he had stuck his leg out to stop him.

How to See Your Angel

CHOPICH said that with practice most of us can learn to see and hear our angels. We hear from our angels often, he said, but we just don't realize it. Angels are very subtle. Often they will put inspirational ideas in our heads. When we accept their guidance, they're happy.

Angels are sad only when we lose our faith in God, or somehow feel unworthy of God's love. During those times, our guardian angels can be a wonderful bridge to God. Each time we pray, our angels pray with us. Our angels constantly encourage us to develop spiritually.

We need to think of guardian angels as our best friends, Chopich said. That includes talking to our angels every day.

Don't try too hard, she said. It's not like praying, for when you pray you close your eyes, concentrate, and send energy to God. If you want to talk to your angel, however, the key is in not trying at all. Keep it light. Praying is energy, but communicating with your angel is frequency. There is a difference. If you try too hard to connect with your angel, your frequency will drop like a rock.

You want to raise your frequency. Your angel will lower his or her frequency so the two of you can connect and communicate. If you raise your frequency even higher, perhaps you can see your angel.

Pick a time of the day when you feel your best. Try to think about your angel while doing little things around the house, like washing dishes, dusting, or mowing the lawn. Keep your thoughts light, almost like a

127

butterfly. Keep your eyes open, because if you close them your frequency will drop. Think of your contact as being like a daydream.

You may start to hear a voice, or feel your angel's presence. You may begin to pick up the ideas your angel puts in your mind. It is all very subtle, but start to listen and eventually you will hear.

Talking with my angel has changed my whole life. I have a peace I never had before. I am happier. I don't worry as much as I used to. I work on my spirituality more. I now know God loves me and I have an angel who is always there for me and thinks I'm wonderful.

HOW TO TALK TO YOUR GUARDIAN ANGEL

Migene Gonzalez-Wippler
(Dec. 2000)

Interacting with your guardian angel doesn't have to be passive, limited to being protected and listening to its advice. Migene González-Wippler, an anthropologist and former editor for the United Nations, shares stories of experiences with her own guardian angels as well as a simple method you can use for talking directly to your own.

IN RECENT YEARS, there have been increasing reports of angel visitations from thousands of people around the world. These experiences range from fleeting visions of angels to actual help from these winged beings, who in many instances are said to have saved people's lives.

Angels can appear in many forms. They may choose to present themselves as ordinary human beings or in the celestial appearance that tradition has given them throughout the centuries: luminous beings with snowy wings, halos and lovely faces, dressed in gossamer tunics, sandaled or barefoot. The hair is usually shoulder-length, golden and curly, and their smiles are always sweet and tender.

Some of the best known angels, like Michael, Gabriel, and Raphael, have been given certain definite characteristics. Michael appears dressed in Roman-type armor, a short tunic, tall Roman sandals, and a flowing red cape draped over his shoulders. In one hand he carries a balance and in the other the sword with which he conquered the Prince of Darkness. Raphael carries a staff and a fish, a symbol of his travels with Tobias. Gabriel holds a lily; symbol of purity during the Annunciation, or a trumpet, a symbol of Judgment Day.

If we are to believe the patriarch Enoch's account, these beings are far from being sweet and gentle looking in their true forms. On the contrary, some of them are so terrifying that they would paralyze a human being with fear. For example, the great angel Kerbela, who is the chief regent of the Cherubim, has a face made of flames, a body made of burning coals, covered with millions of eyes, and eyelashes made of bolts of lightning. He is so tall that his stature surpasses the seven heavens. (Descriptions of many other angels are given in some detail in my book *The Return of the Angels.*)

In reality, angels are spiritual beings, without any physical shape or form. What Enoch tells us about the angelic appearances, and what those—like myself—who have seen angels say about their actual forms is a description of the guise in which the angel chose to appear to these people. Angels may be conceived as cosmic energy, archetypes of the deep unconscious, or emanations of light. But one thing we can be sure of: They are real. They have been with us from our early beginnings and they will be with us until the end of time.

Gabriel

MY MOTHER always told me that the Archangel Gabriel had a special connection with me because he had announced the moment of my birth and had marked me with the sign of the moon, which he rules, according to ancient traditions. I was born at home at 5:35 A.M. According to my mother, reveille was being played at that precise moment at a nearby soldier camp. The midwife told my mother that Gabriel was heralding my entry into the world and that I had something special to do with the angels. Gabriel's instrument is the trumpet and he is one of the angels of life and death.

While she was carrying me, my mother went out one night on the balcony of our house to gaze at the full moon. Inadvertently, she placed her hand on her abdomen, and one of her aunts, who was with her, told her to remove her hand because otherwise the moon was going to mark the child.

My mother took her hand away immediately, but it was too late. When I was born, I had the exact markings of the moon on my left leg, extending toward the hip. As I grew older this mark took less space, but I still have it on my left thigh.

My first experience with an angel happened when my oldest son was born. My obstetrician was Dr. Landrum Shettles, who was the first physician to photograph the human ovum at the moment of fertilization. Dr. Shettles had told us that the baby was due on or around July 4, but this date came and went and the baby was not born. Toward the end of July, Dr. Shettles, now seriously concerned, decided to do a caesarean section. I was brought to the operating room at eleven o'clock in the morning, and several minutes later my son was born without any complications. But immediately after the birth I began to bleed internally. In spite of the efforts of the excellent medical team that was with me at the time, the hemorrhage could not be contained. I sank rapidly into deep shock and the doctors around me began to lose hope of saving my life.

Finally, in desperation, Dr. Shettles decided to call one of his colleagues—the obstetrician who had delivered Elizabeth Taylor's daughter, Liza Todd, also through a caesarean. This doctor, Anthony de Sopo, lived in New Jersey and, because of the gravity of the situation, there was no time for him to travel to New York (where I was) to join Dr. Shettles and the other doctors in the operating room. Therefore he was forced to give detailed instructions to Dr. Shettles over the telephone on the procedure he was to follow to try and stop the bleeding. This treatment had not been used in obstetrics for many years but it was the only hope the doctors had to save my life. Dr. Shettles followed the recommendations of this great doctor and was able to stop the hemorrhage. Thanks to them I am still alive, for which I will always be grateful.

At around six o'clock in the evening I regained consciousness. I struggled through a great, black void from a place very far away. When I opened my eyes I was still in the operating room, and directly above my head was the face of an angel, who smiled tenderly at me. His hair was the palest gold and surrounded his head like a radiant halo. The impression I received was so powerful that I began to sob uncontrollably. The image disappeared at once, and I found myself once more on the operating table, surrounded by many doctors and nurses, all of them happy and relieved because they had been able to save my life. Where did I go while I was unconscious? Was I in Heaven but brought back by the angel to care for my newborn child? I will never know, but I will always remember that beautiful face and its tender, loving smile. This was the first of many experiences with angels.

A Shielding Sword—and a Warning

EIGHT MONTHS after my son was born, my mother came to our house to spend several weeks with us. One afternoon, while my husband was at work, I lay down for a nap with the baby by my side. Some time later my mother entered the room to awaken me, as we had made plans to go shopping. The vision that she saw nearly made her faint in terror.

Standing by the side of the bed was the immense figure of an angel, with widespread wings that nearly reached the ceiling. He was dressed in white armor and Roman sandals and his tunic was short and of a dazzling white. The angel had a large shimmering sword in his hands that he extended protectively over me and the child.

Overcome with awe, but unable to take her eyes away from the vision, my mother walked slowly backward out of the room and closed the door. When she reached her own bedroom, she collapsed on a chair, trembling uncontrollably. Shortly afterward I woke up, and she told me her extraordinary experience. In her opinion, the angel she had seen was the Archangel Michael. From that moment onward, and throughout my life, not only I, but several members of my family, have had profound experiences with Michael.

Many years after my mother's vision of Michael, I had a terrifying experience with the archangel. It happened around six o'clock in the morning, as the sun was beginning to rise. Something awakened me from a deep slumber. I sat in bed, in the grip of a strange foreboding.

I looked through the window at the apartment complex across the way and saw, rising above the building, a gigantic figure that covered all the sky. I saw the white wings and the face of an angel, so bright it was almost impossible to define its features. The figure seemed to be rising with the sun. Somehow I knew it was Michael. Stunned by the sight, I dove under the covers and lay there for a few minutes, trembling with fear. I don't know why I was filled with such dread, but I felt totally overcome with deep anguish, as if something calamitous was about to happen.

After what seemed like an interminable time, I was able to gather enough courage to raise my head from under the sheets and look again at the window. But all I saw was a serene blue sky, gently tinged with the amber rays of the rising sun. The building across from my window was as steadfast and normal as ever, and there was no angel in sight.

I did not report my experience to any member of my family. Later that day, my younger son returned from school with a strange story. He said that as he left the school building, he saw a great angel in the sky with a silver sword in one hand and a balance in the other. He ran all the way home to tell me his vision. As I comforted the child, assuring him that angels are heavenly messengers that can only help and protect us from harm, I had a strong feeling that Michael was trying to tell me that something terrible was about to happen and that I should prepare myself for that moment.

I prayed constantly during the next few weeks, asking for help and protection for myself and my family. Then, just as I had feared, tragedy struck. My mother had a severe, crippling stroke that left her barely clinging to life. For months she remained in the hospital, battling her terrible illness, and during this time she suffered two more strokes. Her illness devastated me. I was an only child and had always been very close to my mother. I did not know how to cope with her condition. I was suddenly immersed in medical decisions, legal considerations, and a host of other problems that left me numb and dazed.

When she was finally released from the hospital, my struggle had just begun. During the 11 years that she lived after her initial illness, she remained in my home, and I cared for her during this time, vainly hoping that she should again be my friend and companion, and my guide in the battles of life. But the stroke had damaged her brain so severely she could barely speak. When she died, I still felt I had failed her somehow, even though her doctor assured me it was time for her to rest. I had not yet learned that death is not an end, but a beginning. This was to be the subject of unrelenting research, finally resulting in my book *What Happens After Death*.

Michael's presence in the sky that fateful day warned me of what was to come. Throughout my entire life, this great archangel has been with me at every moment, letting me feel his presence when I need him the most. His is the voice that sustains and guides me and helps me make the most important decisions in my life.

Writing the Angels

I WILL DESCRIBE a ritual that is done to contact the archangel on the date of your birthday. My father, who was a very religious and mystical man, gave me the ritual—which came to him during meditation—more than 20 years ago. Psalm 85, which was written by Michael (according to tradition), is said to be a powerful aid in contacting the archangel if it is read at night before going to sleep.

Perhaps because of his great asceticism, my father received many revelations from the angels. I would like to share with you two of these angelic messages. The first is a prayer to God written in the form of an acrostic using the first and last names of the person. This prayer must be created by the individual, in a spontaneous form, as it comes from his or her own heart. This prayer will then become that individual's personal prayer to the Creator. Later the prayer is rewritten in the Thebian angelic script below, sealed, and kept in a safe place. To illustrate how such a letter may be composed, I will give a simple example.

a   b   c   d   e   f

g   h   i   k   l   m

n   o   p   q   r   s

t   v   x   y   z

If a person named Ann Smith wished to write a letter to God using her name, she could write it in the following manner.

A lmighty God,

N ever have you ceased to love me.

N one of my prayers have you left unanswered.

S ave me from my own weaknesses and constant doubts.

M ay your mercy follow me always.

I n your light may I walk all the days of my life,

T o find peace, love and the serenity to fulfill my destiny.

H allowed be your name forever.

This prayer would then be transcribed into the angelic script and sealed in an envelope. The original would be used as a personal daily prayer to God. This is only one example of the many prayers that can be composed using a person's name.

The second angelic revelation that I want to give you here was received by my father from the Archangel Michael. It is a petition to Michael and is extremely effective. This letter must be written to Michael only once a year, on your birthday. There can only be one thing asked of the archangel and the letter must be short and very clear as to its intention. To write it, you must have fasted, and abstained from alcohol, drugs, tobacco, and sexual activity, for 24 hours.

Once these preliminaries are observed, write the letter on an unlined piece of white paper. Then place a small glass with a little water in front of yourself and soak a piece of red cloth in the water so that all the liquid is immediately absorbed into the cloth. The red cloth is then placed over your eyes and you may proceed to meditate on the petition to Michael. When some of the water has evaporated from the cloth, both the letter and the cloth are placed in an envelope and sealed. The envelope is addressed to Michael Arch, and below the archangel's name is written the capital and the country that are directly opposite to the country where you were born. (For perfect accuracy, this is ascertained by using the nearest longitude and latitude of both countries. This information can be found in any atlas.) The letter must have a return address and must be certified to ensure its return to the sender. When the letter is returned by the postal authorities of the other country, it is a sign that Michael received the message.

When I wrote such a petition to Michael for the first time, I sent the letter to Karachi, Pakistan, because the opposite longitude and latitude of Puerto Rico, where I was born, are in the middle of the Indian Ocean and I thought that Karachi was the place closest to that specific area. I did not realize at the time that there are many small islands in the Indian Ocean and that the closest to the correct longitude and latitude was the island of Mauritius. My petition to Michael had been to hear from a Norwegian friend with whom I had lost contact for a long time.

Shortly after the postal authorities in Karachi returned Michael's letter, I received a letter from my friend, sent from Mauritius. What was a Norwegian doing in Mauritius, of all places? My friend said that he was on a holiday cruise and the ship had to change its course and dock in the small island because of bad weather. What made him write that letter from Mauritius after such a long silence I will never know. What I do know is that Michael answered my petition and, in so doing, also let me know where to send him any future letters.

How to Learn the Name of Your Guardian Angel

BECAUSE the angel is a cosmic entity of great power it is always advisable to prepare mentally and physically before contacting him. This is not superstition but simple logic. All the energy that is released from the unconscious must be as pure as possible in order to use it effectively.

Bathing and dressing in white are advised because white is a symbol of light which comprises the entire solar spectrum. The burning of incense, specially frankincense and myrrh, aids in concentration, as does the use of soft and ethereal music during the ritual.

To learn the name of your guardian angel, open a previously chosen book, which may be the Bible or a dictionary. The ritual is conducted facing the east, which represents the positive and creative forces of the universe. After the book is opened, close your eyes and place your index finger on the right-hand page. On a piece of white unlined paper, proceed to write down the first letter of the word directly under your finger.

This is repeated three, four, or five times, depending upon your intuition. If you decide to open the book three times, you will write down three letters; if you open the book four times, you will write down four letters; if you open the book five times, you will write down five letters.

Most of the letters you will jot down will be consonants because there are more consonants than vowels in the alphabet. If the letters are all consonants, choose any of the five vowels (a, e, i, o, u) in the order dictated by your own intuition, to place between any of the consonants. If the letters are a combination of vowels and consonants, you may or may not add any more vowels, again according to your intuition. After you have done this, add the termination EL or ON to the letters because most of the angelic names end with one of these two suffixes. Well-known examples of angel names ending in EL or ON are Michael, Gabriel, Raphael, Uriel, Sopheriel, Metraton, and Sandalphon.

For example, if you decide to open the book three times and the letters you jot down are H-R-M, you may decide to add two As and one I to form the name HARAMI. To this, add the termination EL and the angelic name you have created will be HARAMIEL. That is the name of your guardian angel, revealed to you by the angel himself through your own intuitive powers. On the other hand, if you chose to open the book five times, and the letters you wrote down were D-G-A-L-U, you may decide to add only the vowel I to form the name DIGALU, to which you add the termination EL to form DIGALUEL. This will then be the name of your guardian angel. Conversely, you may decide to use the termination ON instead of EL, and the name would then be DIGALUON. If four letters are chosen, like A-T-R-Z, you may decide to add just the vowel I to form the name ATRIZ, to which you add ON to form ATRIZON or EL to form ATRIZEL.

The vowels chosen and the place where they are to be inserted is decided by you, guided by your own intuition and your guardian angel, who reveals his name in this manner. When the name of the angel is known, thank God and the angels and end the ritual. You are now able to call upon your personal guardian angel at any time you may need his help and protection.

WHAT GUARDIAN ANGELS WANT YOU TO KNOW ABOUT TRAGIC DEATHS

Olga N. Worrall

(April 1964)

If you could talk to guardian angels, what would they say to you? Here is a message they gave to a well-known psychic. It will be of particular interest to those who have had loved ones or friends who have suffered a particularly painful or tragic death.

This article is being written at the behest of the Guardian Angels, who each of us comes into the world with and who watch over us and guide us along life's highways and byways, for the enlightenment and comfort of those who have suffered the loss of a loved one through a serious accident, murder, fire, or some other type of tragic, untimely death.—O.N.W.

WE RECEIVED a long distance telephone call from a friend of ours, a well-known writer of many books and articles, requesting that we make it possible for a couple, whom she had just met and who had suffered a terrible loss, to come to our home for spiritual help.

"I know what a heavy schedule you have and I also know that you do not make a practice of seeing strangers. However, in this case, I ask you please to see these people. They are in the depths of despair …only you and your husband can help them, because of your knowledge of immortality. They have need of your spiritual gifts. Please help them. Their child has suffered terrible death."

Knowing that our friend would not ask us to see persons just to satisfy their curiosity, I promised her that we would see the couple that evening.

At the appointed time I opened the door in response to the ringing of the doorbell and saw, standing before me, the husband and wife, wrapped in an aura of deep sorrow. As we sat discussing the facts of immortality, as all Christians should, the time approached for our period of "Silence for Absent Healing" on behalf of those who request our prayers for their many needs.

After about five minutes of "Silence", I clairvoyantly saw standing before the husband, the spirit of a woman who claimed to be his grandmother. After

I described her to the man, he readily accepted her as his grandmother.

She then proceeded to give the following message:

"Tell my grandson and his wife that they must not crucify themselves with regrets and haunting thoughts of just how much their daughter suffered during the ordeal, When the Guardian Angels realized that they were unable to prevent the child's death, they immediately withdrew the astral body, the seat of sensation, from the physical body, and kept it in a state of soul slumber until all possibility of trauma was passed, and the silver cord was severed. We can liken this to the anesthetic used during a physical operation. Through the use of the drug the astral body is dissociated from the physical body, thereby keeping the physical body free from pain during the operation.

"Where we are unable to prevent a tragic passing from taking place the Spirit Specialists use this method to save the soul from trauma. This was done to your child, she did not suffer, and is unaware of what happened to her physical body. She is well and happy and quite anxious to greet you. Wipe your tears my dear children; God is good and does look after His own, in spite of man's cruelty to man."

The child appeared to my clairvoyant sight in full light, radiant and happy. She called out her girlfriend's name as well as her own. She asked me to give her daddy the following message:

"Please tell daddy that my hair is a bit longer now. He will understand."

The father burst into sobs; the mother joined him.

This message was extremely evidential to the parents as the day before the child's passing she had asked her mother to cut her hair real short. She was reminded that her daddy did not like short hair on her. However, the mother agreed to remove about an inch of the ponytail, then if daddy didn't scold, perhaps another inch could be cut off later. That night daddy did scold!

Further evidence was given by the child that thoroughly convinced the parents that they really were communicating with their beloved daughter.

As the parents were preparing to leave they both agreed that a terrible weight had been lifted from their lives and they were grateful for this Holy Communion with Saints.

I trust that this true story will be of some small comfort to those who have suffered such a loss and have wondered, as these parent did, just how much the victim suffered before the spirit left the body.

What a blessing and mental relief this should be for all of us to know that our Guardian Angels have the power to spare a soul from suffering and trauma.

—O.N.W.

WHAT GUARDIAN ANGELS WANT YOU TO KNOW: SUICIDES AREN'T DAMNED— THEY'RE HEALED

Susan Rushing
(May 2011)

According to some religious belief systems, those who take their own lives are sinners fated to burn in hell. Hence, many people who were close to someone who committed suicide worry about their fate in the afterlife. But the guardian angels who spoke to noted psychic Susan Rushing gave her a much more heartening view of what happens in such cases.

IF YOU take your own life, you are condemned to the eternal fires of hell. That is that. At least that is what I was told by my parents, my church and even an assembly I once attended in junior high school. I remember that assembly as if it happened only yesterday. I was 13 or so, sitting in a dark auditorium, listening to a teenaged boy on a recording. He was sad, at his wit's end, apologizing for the failure that he had been to his friends and parents. At the end of his speech there was a long pause and then a loud bang. It startled us all, and somebody even screamed. Then the lights came up and one of the presenters stood in a single spotlight and said, "That poor boy is now burning forever in hell. That is what happens when you decide to take your own life. You burn in hell."

I still remember the horror I felt and the scenario that played in my mind of him lying in his room and then onto the hysteria of his parents finding him. So, needless to say, they made their point. I remember thinking, even at that age, what a disappointment that God would not take mercy on that sad young man. I bought what they sold, but deep down inside it didn't feel right.

The Gift of Sight

THIRTY years later I would realize that, without a doubt in my mind, it wasn't.

Sometimes gifts come to us in unusual ways. This particular gift

139

came to me in the form of a request for a free reading from an event promoter. The promoter told me that she had a friend who was in a bad place in her life and she felt that I was the one who could help her out. I agreed to the reading, and in my self-centered fear, I felt taken advantage of. Little did I know this reading would turn out to be a bigger gift to me than my small mindedness could have ever imagined at that moment.

I had assumed that this would be another reading of dire questions about some cheating man or quests for predictions of real estate transactions. Imagine my shock when on the other end of the phone line was a sobbing woman whose son had committed suicide just three months before. My head began to spin as I prayed to be given the best information possible for this woman. All the while she was crying and begging me to try to connect with her son. I prayed, "Jesus, if you have ever given me the good stuff, it has to be now. I can't hurt this woman any more than she already hurts."

Without a moment passing, into my vision came a young man with shaggy brown hair. Amazingly, he was being brought forward, almost carried under the arms by two massive angels. I could not believe what I was being shown.

They took him close to me. He looked exhausted, his head hanging down with dark circles under his eyes. He gave me messages for his mother of apology. He had been sick in thought; his mind swirling and swirling for years. He had been addicted to drugs and had recently gotten clean. But being clean made his thoughts begin to swirl again and he said that he just couldn't take it any longer. He told me that he was okay. He also explained that he had work to do and that if his mother needed him, to just ask. His energy was low, but he explained that he could be in several places at a time. I communicated for over an hour, my mind trying to process all of this new and confusing information and give messages to his mother at the same time.

When we ended the reading, the mother seemed to feel better about where her son was and how he was doing. I, on the other hand had some serious questions that would not leave. After all, I believed that once you crossed to the other side it was all love and forgiveness, peace and tranquility. Was there really the harsh punishments and judgments that I had been warned about in my youth? The young man, however, was tired, exhausted. He didn't seem happy or rejuvenated or any of the things that I had imagined would happen when a soul crossed over to the other side. It was perplexing and, not wanting to question what Spirit gives me during my readings, I set it aside in my mind for the rest of the night and well into the next day.

Searching for Answers

W HEN I finally went into meditation, late the next day, I asked for any messages from my guides and angels. I received a small, almost greeting-card-like message. Definitely not a typical message from my usual long-talking guides. I closed my eyes again and focused in and asked why my message was so short. The response I received was, "It is not the answer you truly seek." As usual, they were right. It wasn't what was on my mind. I wasn't really sure I wanted to know the answer to the question. That was pretty deep stuff, and I wasn't sure if I was ready. Then I realized that if I hadn't been ready, my guides would not have been so eager to share the information. So, I took a deep breath and asked, "What were those angels?"

The message I was given was this:

"You are correct in that they are guardians or centauries. They are charged with guarding the souls that come to them for healing. You are incorrect in your thinking of this soul's captivity. This is a situation of protection of the soul.

"There is accountability, but not as you have imagined. Each one must be responsible for the seeing, the feeling and the aiding in the repair of the deficit of energy that they have left in ending their life. They must see the grief that they have caused. They must feel the grief that their loved ones are feeling. As situations arise, it is in their power to be of assistance; they must aid to repair the situation as it is brought before them. It is this accountability. It is all in the realm that you call Heaven. They are in the care and the love of the Father for all time."

The angels had to bring this young man forward during the reading to help him repair some of the deficits that he had left for his mother. They accompanied him because his energy was not strong enough for him to come through on his own, and it was not strong enough to get him back to the other side without assistance.

I was shown a place that suicide victims go to once they cross. It made me think of a hospital. My guides helped me understand that the majority of people who take their life are spiritually ill. They have lost hope and light and are in need of a great deal of love. Special angels were here to surround them with love and healing. They could stay as long as they needed, before continuing their soul's journey in another realm. Some souls stay longer and participate in the healing of others. Some stay for a very long time.

There seemed to be no timetable. It was very quiet and peaceful with soft pink love energy everywhere.

It became clear to me that suicide does not condemn a soul to hell, but neither is it an easy way out.

The work that waits on the other side is clearly supported in love, but seems a long, sad and tiring journey to fix something that should not have been broken. I am hoping as I write this that the young man that came through in my reading is healing well and finding some peace. I pray for the family that he left behind and hope that they are doing the same. Ω

PART V

GUARDIAN ANGELS AT WORK

ITH SEVEN BILLION human beings walking the face of the Earth, one can only imagine how busy guardian angels are kept in keeping a watchful eye over every single one of them. But every single minute of every single day they are on the job, hovering protectively near. Only heaven itself could have or create such powers. The following reports from our readers and contributors reflect the wide variety of their activities in behalf of those to whose care they are assigned.

THE WINDOW THAT WOULDN'T STAY CLOSED

Minnie Alford
(Sept. 1994)

This is an almost textbook case of how guardian angels help people every day. If there is such a thing as "everyday" in the angelic realm, then here is a reader account of the every-day doings of guardian angels.

IN JANUARY 1979, after receiving an $80 December gas bill, my boyfriend, Ruben G. Anaya, and I decided to insulate my house. We were on a fixed income, and raising two children from my previous marriage was hard.

I called a local company and had marble insulation blown into the attic. It really helped. We could feel the difference right away. Shortly afterward, my children and I started to experience nausea and headaches. We had flu-like symptoms for almost a week. We went to see a doctor a couple of times, but he found nothing wrong. It became so bad that I felt something or someone did not want us at home.

Then something strange began to happen. A window in my bedroom would open on its own. I repeatedly closed the window, only to find it open again. And our flu symptoms continued. I finally called my doctor for another appointment and he suggested we have our furnace checked.

I called the gas company immediately. A man came within 20 minutes. He checked my cooking stove and the water heater, and then opened a door located behind the furnace. Quickly he stepped back and said, "Lady, there is enough carbon monoxide in here to kill the whole family. You must have a guardian angel."

I immediately thought of the window in my room. When we checked the furnace vent, we found that some of the insulation had blown into it, completely blocking it. If not for our guardian angel opening the window, I believe we all would have died. By the way, the window no longer opens by itself.

MYSTERY WOMAN OR GUARDIAN ANGEL?

Mary Crawford
(Dec. 2002)

Who comforted the elderly patient as she lay helpless on the floor? The doors of the apartment were all locked. Yet someone had entered and sat silently on the rocking chair, keeping her company through the night.

IN FEBRUARY 2000, I began providing day care for Mrs. U. Hughes, who was 87 and living alone. She is a darling person, and I became very attached to her.

Usually, I would arrive at her home around 7:15 A.M. But on March 29, 2002, I had an uneasy feeling. I left early and arrived about 7:02. The door was locked, and I couldn't hear any sounds from inside. I had a key, so I unlocked the door and let myself in. I found Mrs. Hughes lying in the doorway of her bedroom. She was alert, but she couldn't get up. The strange thing was that she was not moaning or struggling. She seemed perfectly calm.

Since I weigh 110 pounds and she is considerably larger, I did not try to get her up. Instead, I phoned for help. Having completed my phone call, I came back and sat down beside her, thinking that I could comfort her until help arrived.

"Where did that woman go?" asked Mrs. Hughes.

I asked her whom she was talking about. She stated that she didn't know who she was, nor how she got inside.

"What did she say to you?" I asked.

Mrs. Hughes told me that whoever the woman was, she was not anyone she knew. And that she never told her name nor even said a word. "She just pulled up a chair and sat down beside me!" Mrs. Hughes elaborated, "I could tell that she was a good person and that she wanted to help me."

Since I had unlocked the door myself, I knew that no one else had been there. So I suggested that perhaps it was Mrs. Hughes's guardian angel, who came to watch over her until I arrived. Mrs. Hughes just smiled and said, "You know, it might have been."

Some believe in guardian angels; others do not. I think this being was her guardian angel. Mrs. Hughes was far too calm and collected for any other explanation.

THE BACK 40

Martha Sherman
(Dec. 1993)

In this personal account, reader Martha Sherman describes a very rare kind of experience when she is protected from death by being actually picked up in the arms of her guardian angel. It all happened on. . .

IN 1942, my husband Harold Sherman and I purchased 120 acres of rugged Arkansas hill property, only to discover that the back 40 had been formed by the long forgotten series of devastating earthquakes in 1811-12. These quakes had violently shaken northeastern Arkansas, southeastern Missouri, western Kentucky and northwestern Tennessee, and several other eastern states. This area has since been called the New Madrid Fault, said to have been the scene of the most turbulent earth disturbances ever recorded on this continent.

The back 40 was extremely picturesque, with its jumble of rocky drop-offs where huge portions of rock islands had been broken off from solid, nearby stone precipices.

In the more than 180 years since the New Madrid quake, trees and rugged growth have emerged from cracks in these gigantic forms, adding to their rustic beauty.

I had taken much pleasure clearing and maintaining a path all along this bluff area, where my husband and I would occasionally take interested guests. Often, I went back there by myself when I knew my husband would be busy for several hours at his typewriter.

One day, while making my way home, I had to cross a stream that led into the upper level of a waterfall cascading 35 feet over a rocky ledge to the forest floor below. I prepared to jump over some stepping stones, a distance of five feet to the other side, as I had done countless times before. Suddenly my foot slipped, and in one terrifying moment I visualized myself lying badly injured at the bottom of these precipitous falls, helpless, until some hours later when I might be missed and discovered.

But, miraculously, this did not happen. Instead, I felt myself caught in mid-air, spun gently around and deposited as lightly as a feather on the very same rock from which I had just started.

I lay there for a moment in a daze, trying to think how this astounding thing could possibly have happened—memories came flooding back to me of long ago when, as a school girl on my way back to class, I had felt myself lifted softly into the air (in much the same way) and set down gently some 20 feet farther on the sidewalk, for no apparent reason. I had briefly thought that perhaps it was to show me that these things were possible. But I then decided it must have been a figment of my imagination and had said nothing to anyone else about it. I was sure no one would have believed me anyway.

However, this was now. I knew what had just happened. I could only conclude that some unseen presence, a guardian angel or protector, had intervened and come to my rescue.

It took a lot of courage to attempt the crossing once more, but fortified by the protective help I had just received, I tried again and arrived on the other side of the stream in complete safety.

Was I being warned that I should never come here alone after this? Whether that was the purpose or not, I have never returned alone to this day. And other than a few close friends and family, I have never shared this true story until this moment. It is my hope that, at 94, my story might give courage to others in times of *crisis*.

GUARDIAN ANGEL IN THE LAND OF THE CZARS

Eugene Mamtchitch
(Translated by Susy Smith)
(Nov. 1961)

Seventy years before the preceding anecdote took place; a Russian judge was also protected from certain death by his own guardian angel, Palladia, in an incident told in his own words and expertly translated by the world famous psychic and author, Susy Smith.

UNIQUE in the annals of psychic research is this account of an apparition which seemed to have continuing knowledge of the affairs of her friend on earth. Frederick W. H. Myers printed this entire letter along with additional testimony in the original French in his epic study, *Human Personality*. The portion of the letter published here is from a translation prepared by Susy Smith, the study's most recent editor.

Monsieur,

My guardian angel, Palladia, was the daughter of a wealthy Russian landlord. Her father died a few months before she was born, and her mother soon sent her away to a convent.

In 1872, Palladia was being sent from the convent to the Crimea for health reasons. I was called upon by Palladia's brother in an effort to get her back into society against her own desire. I did my best to help the brother, and that is when I met Palladia for the first time.

She was 14, tall, thin and already suffering from tuberculosis. At the brother's request, I accompanied Palladia and her sister to Crimea where they were to spend the winter, and remained two weeks with them.

In 1873, by chance I met Palladia and her sister at Odessa, where they had come to see some doctors, although Palladia looked in better health. On August 27, while I was reading to the ladies, Palladia died suddenly of an aneurysm; she was 15.

At a séance two years after Palladia's death I heard raps, and thought it was a joke. But at home, I wanted to see if the same raps would be repeated and settled myself in the same position I had assumed at the séance.

Through the alphabet, I communicated with Palladia. She said, "Replace the angel, it is falling."

I visited her grave, and found a marble statue of an angel had fallen to the side of her grave. I replaced it.

A year after Palladia sent this message, she appeared to me for the first time. It was October, 1876, and I was in Kieff, playing the piano in the apartment of a friend. Suddenly I saw Palladia, and my friend came to ask me what had happened. He thought that it must have been the servant, but we were alone in the apartment.

Now I see her often. Sometimes three times a week, sometimes twice in the same day, sometimes a month goes by.

She always appears unexpectedly, when I don't think of her. When I do think of her, or try to see her, she never appears.

She always appears in the same manner, with a serene expression. She always appears in the dark dress in which she died under my eyes. I see her when I'm alone and when I have company.

The apparition remains one, two, three minutes, and then gradually vanishes into space.

Palladia has appeared to my son, and may have visited my wife, even before I myself knew that she was to be my bride.

This took place in 1885. I was alone with my dog in a room at my parents' when Palladia appeared, five steps away from me, with a joyful smile. She approached me and said, "I went. I, saw." Then she disappeared.

My setter yelped and jumped on my bed. I didn't speak to anyone about this, but the evening of the same day a young woman visiting in my parents' house told me, "When I woke up this morning I felt someone near my bed and heard a voice say, 'Don't be scared of me, I am good and affectionate.'"

I did not tell this young lady anything of my own experiences until a year later, when I was engaged to her. At the time of the apparition, I had no idea of getting engaged to this lady, it was in fact, the first time I had seen her.

I wonder whether it was Palladia who also had stopped by the bed of my future wife?

Five years later I was with my wife and two-year-old son, staying with friends in the country. One evening about seven P.M., I was sitting in a room lighted by a big lamp. The door opened and my son came running to me. Suddenly Palladia appeared before me. I turned toward my son. He was looking at Palladia; he pointed to her and turned to me saying, "The aunt." I took him on my knees and turned toward Palladia, but she had gone. My son's face was peaceful and happy.

THE GUARDIAN ANGEL WHO SAVED THE *ESSEX*

Anonymous Crew Member
(Feb. 2000)

There have been multitudes of stories about the miraculous appearance of guardian angels to aid individuals, platoons, aircraft and ships during time of war. The following history was adapted with permission from an authentic personal account that appears on NavyHistory.com.

THE EXPERIENCES of the USS *Essex* were among the most fantastic in World War II. The *Essex* destroyed more Japanese planes and enemy ships than any other ship afloat during the war. She received the Presidential Unit Citation, but that was not the most amazing thing about her.

If there ever was anything in this world to prove the existence of a guardian angel, the story of the *Essex* proves it beyond all doubt.

I was lucky to be on that ship through the war. She was the only carrier to last throughout the war. At the close of the war, she was under constant attack for three months—the longest period she was not firing at enemy aircraft during that three months was ten minutes. Frequently we were alone for days or weeks until another carrier or two could be brought in.

She was in every important battle after the Coral Sea.

At the very beginning of her duty, she was in the raid at Rabaul. That's the first time she showed her "luck." During that attack by more than 400 Japanese aircraft, she made a turn to avoid five torpedoes. The turn exceeded her design capability—she went far past the capsize point and raced between three torpedoes on one side and two on the other side. They went the full length of the ship right next to it. When we leveled up, it seemed to take forever and she shuddered like she was being beaten, but she came back.

We saw much battle. One time, three "Betty" aircraft dropped two torpedoes each at point blank range. Too close to miss. Topsiders braced for the hit. The two middle torpedoes hit the water and exploded on contact. The two forward torpedoes hit the water and bounced, came down, angled off the bow, and missed. The two aft torpedoes hit the water, bounced, and came down and angled off the fantail.

The escapes go on and on. The single time she was hit by a *kamikaze*, a photo from another ship shows the suicide plane making a near right angle turn in its dive—just over the rear of the flight deck, which was loaded with a full strike, bombs, rockets, gel bombs, the works, and hitting forward of the gun mounts. We were back in action in minutes, instead of having sixty burning combat aircraft blowing up. The *kamikaze* was already short one wing when it made that turn.

The only other time the *Essex* was hit was with a large bomb below the waterline. It hit in a void space designed to protect the vitals of the ship. We operated for months with a hole you could drive a semi through until we could break off long enough for a quick repair trip to the States, and even then it was really an emergency trip to pick up a division of Marines to replace a division that had just been wiped out.

The *Essex* had more than one admiral made on her. The Japanese proudly announced that they had sunk her. Her escapes were legendary.

Angels Are Real

AT ONE POINT her crew had it brought home to them that guardian angels are real.

A crewman from the USS *Bunker Hill* was brought on board for a few hours during transshipment to the U.S.: His story came with him over the radio. They said that he had been on the *Bunker Hill* since the first time she was in action. He had been on various work assignments on the *Bunker Hill*. Unfortunately, he was unable to handle any work he was tried on—even unable to be a compartment cleaner, so they decided to send him back to the States. When he was told he was being sent back, he tried to refuse the transfer, went into a panic, said that the luck of the *Bunker Hill* was riding with him and told all his ship mates not to send him. He said that if he was forced to leave, the *Bunker Hill* would be badly hit within 48 hours. Up to that point in time, the *Bunker Hill* and the *Essex* had already been through hell together. They had to force him off the *Bunker Hill*. It was about eighteen hours later that the *Bunker Hill* was badly hit.

Those of us on the *Essex* wondered which one of us was being guarded by the Creator, but whoever it was, he never came forward. And no matter who it was, I was glad to be on his ship.

Hollywood Hero

THERE WAS a movie star on board for a while. His name was Wayne Morris and he was a fighter pilot. The often-decorated Morris flew 57 combat missions and shot down seven enemy planes. If any one man ever could have been responsible for winning a major battle, it was he. In fact, his term in the service crippled his movie career; after the war, his roles were confined to B pictures.

It was in the early morning of the day before the second battle of the Philippine Seas, the last really big battle of the American and Japanese fleets, the one that broke the back of the Japanese navy.

All night we had hunted for the Japanese fleet and finally our new night fighters located it. At dawn we had a full strike after them and they were not expecting us. Morris had a 500 pounder and he went into their fleet and searched until he found their only "ready" carrier. Then he sat up there in the air in all that hell until the forward elevator went down. Then Morris dove down and wrecked the elevator in the down position. Unable to get fighters into the air, that was the end of the Japanese fleet. Morris never got the credit due him. His real life even surpassed his movie roles.

UFO Visits USS Essex

ANOTHER ITEM that was never reported: Near the end of the war we were visited by a UFO. It was after we had destroyed the Japanese fleet. We had the ocean all to ourselves.

So here we are, battleships and cruisers, destroyers and carriers, all in a tight group. Bright clear day. Radar reports a bogey coming in on us at 40,000 feet and 4,000 miles per hour. So we were waiting. The UFO made a right angle drop over us and came down at 4,000 miles per hour. It stopped dead in the air about 20 feet off the water on the port bow of the fleet. It just hung there, point blank range, pacing the fleet. Everything we had was firing at it, and not missing.

It was sitting right in front of a battleship and the 16-inch shells were hitting it at point blank range. Everything was exploding 50 feet away from the craft and it ignored them. It was spherical and about 100 feet in diameter. After a few minutes, it started moving at about 15 to 20 miles per hour, on a sightseeing trip. It made a water level tour of the fleet. Down the side, across the rear, up the right side, to the same area on the starboard side. It sat there a few more minutes then went up from a standing start at 4,000 miles per hour, another right angle turn at 4,000 miles per hour back the way it came. All the time we were shelling it and not missing. When they started to log the event, orders were given that it was only "an unidentified bogey."

Crew Can Verify

MOST of the men on board the *Essex* stayed with her through the war, other than the air groups, one of which lost about 90 percent of the initial group in combat. You could locate much of the crew by use of the new government chapters. All of this, plus much more, will verify the charmed life of the ship and can be documented.

It just seems to me that the story should be told, that the world should know that sometimes, for reasons that only He knows, the Creator will step forward into the affairs of humanity and change things to His own satisfaction.

A History of the Essex

THE FOURTH *ESSEX* (CV-9) was launched July 31, 1942 by Newport News Shipbuilding and Dry Dock Co. sponsored by Mrs. Artemus L. Gates, wife of the Assistant Secretary of the Navy for Air; and commissioned December 31, 1942, Capt. D. B. Duncan commanding. She was reclassified CVA-9 on October 1, 1952, and CVS-9 on March 8, 1960.

Following her shakedown cruise, the *Essex* sailed to the Pacific in May 1943 to begin a series of victories that would bring her to Tokyo Bay. Departing Pearl Harbor, she participated with Task Force (TF) 15 in carrier operations against Marcus Island (August 31, 1943), was designated flagship of TF 14 and struck Wake Island (October 5-6), launched an attack with Task Group (TG) 50.3 against the Gilbert Islands, where she also took part in her first amphibious assault, the landing on Tarawa (November 18-23). Refueling at sea, she cruised as flagship of TG 50.3 to attack Kwajalein (December 4). Her second amphibious assault delivered in company with TG 58.2 was against the Marshalls (January 29—February 2, 1944).

The *Essex* in TG 58.2 now joined with TG 58.1 and 58.3 to constitute the most formidable carrier striking force to date in launching an attack against Truk (February 17-18), during which eight Japanese ships were sunk. In route to the Marianas to sever Japanese supply lines, the carrier force was detected and received a prolonged aerial attack, which it repelled in a businesslike manner, and then continued with the scheduled attack upon Saipan, Tinian, and Guam (February 23).

After this operation, the *Essex* proceeded to San Francisco for her single wartime overhaul. She then joined carriers *Wasp* (CV-18) and *San Jacinto* (CVL30) in TG 12.1 to strike Marcus Island (May 19-20) and Wake (May 23). She deployed with TF 58 to support the occupation of the Marianas (June 12—August 10); sortied with TG 38.3 to lead an attack against the Palau Islands (September 6-8), and Mindanao (September 9-10), with enemy shipping as the main target, and remained in the area to support landings on Peleliu. On October 2, she weathered a typhoon and four days later departed with TF 38 for the Ryukyus.

For the remainder of 1944, she continued her front-line action, participating in strikes against Okinawa (October 10) and Formosa (October 12-14), covering the Leyte landings, taking part in the battle for Leyte Gulf (October 24-25) and continuing the search for enemy fleet units until October 30, when she returned to Ulithi, Caroline Islands, for replenishment. She resumed the offensive and delivered attacks on Manila and the northern Philippine Islands during November. On November 25, for the first time in her far-ranging operations and destruction to the enemy, the *Essex* received injury. A *kamikaze* hit the port edge of her flight deck, landing among planes gassed for takeoff and causing extensive damage, killing 15 and wounding 44.

This cramped her style very little. Following quick repairs, we find her with the Third Fleet off Luzon supporting the occupation of Mindoro (December 14-16). She rode out the typhoon of December 18 and made a special search for survivors afterward. With TG 38.3, she participated in the Lingayen Gulf operations, launched strikes against Formosa, Sakishima, Okinawa, and Luzon. Entering the South China Sea in search of enemy surface forces, the task force pounded shipping and conducted strikes on Formosa, the China coast, Hainan, and Hong Kong. The *Essex* withstood the onslaught of the third typhoon in four months (January 20-21, 1945) before striking again at Formosa, Miyako Shima, and Okinawa (January 26-27).

During the remainder of the war, she operated with TF 58, conducting attacks against the Tokyo area (February 16-17 and 25), both to neutralize the enemy's air power before the landings on Iwo Jima and to cripple the aircraft manufacturing industry. She sent support missions against Iwo Jima and neighboring islands, but from March 23 to May 28, was employed primarily to support the conquest of Okinawa.

In the closing days of the war, the *Essex* took part in the final telling raids against the Japanese home islands (July 10-August 15). Following the surrender, she continued defensive combat air patrols until September 3, when she was ordered to Bremerton, Washington, for inactivation. On January 9, 1947, she was placed out of commission in reserve.

Modernization endowed the *Essex* with a new flight deck and a streamlined island superstructure on January 15, 1951, when re-commissioned, Capt. A.W. Wheeloek commanding.

After a brief cruise in Hawaiian waters she began the first of three tours in Far Eastern waters during the Korean war. She served as flagship of Carrier Division 1 and TF 77. She was the first carrier to launch F2H "Banshee" twin-jet fighters on combat missions; on September 16, 1951, one of these planes, damaged in combat, crashed into aircraft parked on the forward flight deck, causing an explosion and fire that killed seven. After repairs at Yokosuka, she returned to front-line action on October 3 to launch strikes up to the Yalu River and provide close air support for U.N. troops.

On December 1, 1953, she started her final tour of the war, sailing the China Sea with the Peace Patrol. From November 1954 to June 1955, she engaged in training exercises, operated for three months with the Seventh Fleet, assisted in the Tachen Islands evacuation, and engaged in air operations and fleet maneuvers off Okinawa.

In July 1955, the *Essex* entered Puget Sound Naval Shipyard for repairs and extensive alterations, including installation of an angled flight deck. Modernization completed, she rejoined the Pacific Fleet in March 1956. For the next 14 months, the carrier operated off the West Coast, except for a six-month cruise with the Seventh Fleet in the Far East. Ordered to join the Atlantic Fleet for the first time in her long career, she sailed from San Diego on June 21,1957, rounded Cape Horn, and arrived in Mayport, Florida, on August 1.

In the fall of 1957, the *Essex* participated as an antisubmarine carrier in the NATO exercises "Strike Back;' and in February 1958 deployed with the Sixth Fleet until May, when she shifted to the eastern Mediterranean. Alerted to the Middle East crisis on July 14, 1958, she sped to support the U.S. Peace Force, landing in Beirut, Lebanon, launching reconnaissance and patrol missions until August 20. Once again she was ordered to proceed to Asian waters and transited the Suez Canal to arrive in the Taiwan operational area, where she joined TF 77 in conducting flight operations before rounding the Horn and proceeding back to Mayport.

The *Essex* joined with the Second Fleet and British ships in Atlantic exercises and with NATO forces in the eastern Mediterranean during the fall of 1959. In December she aided victims of a disastrous flood at Frejus, France.

In the spring of 1960, she was converted into an ASW Support Carrier and was thereafter home-ported at Quonset Point, Rhode Island. Since that time she has operated as flagship of Carrier Division 18 and Antisubmarine Carrier Group Three. She conducted rescue and salvage operations off the New Jersey coast for a downed blimp, cruised with midshipmen, and was deployed on NATO and CENTO exercises. In November 1960, she joined the French navy in Operation "Jet Stream," and after that time continued her widespread activities in the protection of freedom and peace.

The *Essex* received the Presidential Unit Citation and 13 battle stars for WW II service, and four battle stars and the Navy Unit Commendation for Korean War service.

HOW A GUARDIAN ANGEL SAVED MY LIFE

Boczor Iosif
(August 1996)

On the other side of the World during that same war Boczor Iosif, a Transylvanian writer for European paranormal publications found himself also under the protective wing of a guardian angel.

I LIVED in Satu Mare, a city in Northern Transylvania in the 1940s. This important railway junction belonged to Hungary between 1940-1944. In March 1944 the Germans occupied Hungary. Satu Mare also had a German military commandment.

On a hot May day, about 10:00 A.M., I was playing alone on the roadside near our house. My father was working at the post office and my mother was at the market. Suddenly I observed a cart full with people, wearing a yellow star. I had no idea why they were wearing it and what fate was waiting for them.

A 15-year-old boy told the Hungarian gendarmes that I was a Jew. When the cruel, unscrupulous gendarmes grabbed me, I did not resist because I thought it was fun for me to travel by a cart.

One of our neighbors, Miss Templom ran out the street and told the gendarmes "Let this little boy go because his parents are Christian."

I had made several steps towards Auschwitz. I am firmly convinced that Miss Church was my guardian angel.

Earlier, in 1938, my father, Boczor Jozsef, gave his name to a friend, Bocow Wolff, a chemical engineer. This Jewish Hungarian engineer went to Spain in 1938 then in 1940 to France, using the name of Jozsef Boczor. He was a fighter of the French Liberation Army. He led the detachment specialized in derailing SS and Wehrmacht trains. He was a specialist in explosives. On February 21, 1944, he was executed by the Germans at Mont Valerien, together with other fighters. At the beginning of February my father had a vision of his Jewish friend in a pool of blood, near a wall.

In the middle of September 1944, Satu Mare was hit by pattern bombing of the Allies: America, English and Russian planes.

"Today we escape from this earthly hell to a small island of peace, Baia

Sprie," my father told me, my mother and my sister after a pattern bombing.

Baia Sprie is a small town 70 km from Satu Mare.

The next day we started out to the railway station at 7:30 P.M. The railway station was about 700 meters from our house. At the station we were informed that the train only went on the following day to Baia Mare.

We started back immediately to our house but our father stopped suddenly on the way.

"I hear the voice of my uncle's spirit. He whispers to me that after half an hour a train with two carriages would start to Baia Mare," he told us.

We turned around without hesitation. At the railway station we would find out that my uncle's spirit had told the truth.

When the sirens began to howl, our train had already left the station.

We arrived to Baia Sprie about 11 o' clock. Our grandparents lovingly embraced us. In that safe environment, I then dreamt about faeries dancing on a clearing of an oakwood near my grandparents' small house.

A week later, on his return, my father was shocked because he discovered that the air-raid shelter of our courtyard was collapsed. He found out from his neighbor that it had been hit while we were traveling to Baia Mare.

About three weeks later while I was leafing through pictures in in my grandparents' sitting room, my mother and grandmother were talking about ordinary things like good cooking in peacetime. Suddenly the sleepy silence was broken by the rattle of the windows. Simultaneously the doors opened by themselves. For some moments we stood rooted to the spot, then we ran out into the courtyard. We did not see any people or animals there, and on that starlit, calm evening we could have heard a single apple fall onto the grassy ground.

After we went back into the house, my grandmother looked at the old cuckoo clock. "It is five past eight," she told us.

Next day, at two P.M. the postman gave a telegram to my grandparents. According to this telegram, their son had died unexpectedly at seven o'clock, the previous evening in Cluj, a city about 200 km from Baia Sprie.

Later, in the '90s, on a cloudy July evening in Budapest I had been talking with the editors of a Hungarian journal in a restaurant until about 11:00 P.M... I wanted to go to my lodgings by underground, but I changed my mind because an inner voice advised me to call a taxi. I follow my guardian angel's advice.

The next day I found out from a newspaper that the previous evening a passer-by had been beaten and robbed in the park near my lodgings.

THE TEEN DRIVER AND THE GUARDIAN ANGEL

Ian P. Harris
(Sept. 1968)

Ten years later, in Britain, in peacetime, guardian angels where still on the spot when an English lad had the following uncanny experience which he shared with other readers of Fate.

WHEN I was a young man living in Bedfordshire, England, two incidents which occurred in my 18th year made me acutely aware of invisible forces which in times of stress or need can—and often do—affect our lives. One bitterly cold night in November, 1937, my friend Bob Burton and I had collected our friends, Phyllis Jackson and Joyce Reardon, in the village of Barton to take them to a movie in Luton, a few miles south of Bedford. A light dust of snow was falling, making the icy roads even more hazardous. Because the movie lasted much longer than we had anticipated, we felt we had to hurry to get the girls home.

In retrospect I realize that the return journey that winter's night was my first trip into the unknown. We were about a half mile from the intersection where I would turn toward the village of Barton when the car started to slow down—quite forcefully. It felt for all the world as if the brakes were being applied. The car pulled so hard that I had to shift into low gear to make the turn. Ahead of me stretched a fairly steep downgrade of icy road for perhaps a mile and a half or two miles. Quickly I shifted into high, thinking I would make up for lost time on the downhill run regardless of the icy road. To my surprise, instead of going faster, the car moved more and more slowly.

I knew this road very well and normally I should be able to coast down the hill at 40 or 45 miles an hour with the engine switched off and the gears in neutral. Angrily I shifted down to second and when the car wouldn't pull in that gear I slammed it into low. Without realizing how silly it was, I seemed to be trying mentally to force the car to do my bidding.

Suddenly I thought, "I'm out of oil and the engine is going to seize up!" The oil gauge didn't work so I had no way of knowing if the oil pressure had fallen. Quickly I switched the ignition off and shifted into neutral. If I could coast to the bottom of the hill I could get some oil.

When I moved the stick into neutral the car suddenly stopped—as if I had jammed on the brakes. Reflexively I put my foot on the brake pedal to hold the car while I tried to figure out what was wrong.

"Hey, Pete!" Bob's voice came from behind me. "What on earth are you stopping here for? Why don't you let the car coast down the hill?"

When I turned to answer him I inadvertently released the pressure on the brake pedal and to my utter amazement the car started backing up the hill with increasing speed. I was petrified for ten or 15 seconds until one of the girls let out a terrified scream. The sudden shock made me slam on the brakes again.

The car stopped with a jerk and we all sat there in a frozen silence punctuated only by the eerie sound of the whistling wind and the faint noises of the falling snow.

Then, in a detached sort of way, I noticed a gradual bend in the road about a half mile ahead. Coming around it was a big truck. We all watched in horror as it skidded broadside across the road, straightened up and skidded again before the driver regained control. It roared past us in a blaze of headlights. After it had gone by, I realized that if my car had not been stationary I certainly should have smashed into the truck as it careened around that bend.

After a few moments I decided I might as well try to start the car. With shaking fingers I switched on the ignition and pressed the starter button. The engine burst into life and I carried on down the road without the slightest bother.

A few minutes later we were in Barton where we left the girls at their homes. During the remainder of the trip to Millbrook, where Bob lived, I don't think either of us spoke a word. When I said goodnight he just stared at me vacantly and walked into his house, I went on to Bedford. I didn't tell either Mother or Father about what had happened. They would have thought me quite mad—and I might have had a little trouble getting to keep my car. I decided to try to forget the whole incident—but that wasn't in the cards.

A few weeks later my mother showed me an article about a London séance, saying, "I've always wanted to go to one of these. If I can make a booking, will you come with me?"

I laughed at her but with youth's élan I said, "You bet I will but it's bound to be a fake."

The letter she wrote gave no personal details beyond saying we were

THE TEEN DRIVER AND THE GUARDIAN ANGEL

interested in psychic matters and asking for a booking. In due course a reply came notifying us that the séance would be the London suburb of Hampton Court at 2:30 P.M. on a date two weeks hence.

When the day arrived I duly drove Mother to London and then to Hampton Court where we located the house without any trouble. It was quite an ordinary house, not a bit like the bat-infested place I had seen in a horror movie the night before.

We were greeted at the door by a charming woman who proved to be the medium, Louisa Bolt. She showed us into the lounge where three other people sat. A few minutes later another woman arrived and we were taken into the séance room.

In the subdued blue lighting I made out a round table surrounded by chairs for the sitters in the center of the carpeted floor. On the table was a stand bearing a vertical piece of metal or wood. At its point rested what looked like a crosspiece with little cones at its ends. The cones were luminous and in the subdued light they glowed with a greenish radiance. I noticed the entire crosspiece revolved on the center point.

Mrs. Bolt invited us to inspect the room to satisfy ourselves there were no hidden wires or gadgets anywhere. When this had been done we sat down at the table. The lights were lowered a little more but we still could see each other. First we sang a hymn and slowly the cones started to revolve. In a few moments voices seemed to come from them.

This meant very little to me. I was not at all involved but I did notice that the people who were addressed seemed to recognize the voices. It was like eavesdropping on long-distance telephone conversations.

This went on for about an hour and then from the center of the hushed room a rich Irish voice boomed out, "I'll be speaking to the gentleman sitting all by himself."

In a weak voice I said, "Me?"

"Sure, 'tis yourself I want to speak to. You know, when I was on the earth plane I was a rare one for speed. I had an old motorcycle and one day when I was racing down the road, as I liked to do, I came to a corner and on that corner was a pond. Sure and I was over here before I knew it just like you would have been if we had not pushed you backwards up that hill to stop you meeting the truck on the corner." Then speaking to my mother the voice added, "Never fear, lady, I'll always watch over him when he drives."

Needless to say, I was shaken up—not the least by the tall explaining I had to do on the ride home with Mother. The drive home was otherwise uneventful—but within a few weeks a second, even stranger event was to occur.

On a very dark night in al January, a friend who lived in Stewartby, called around and suggested we go over to Rushden, a town a few miles west of Bedford. We walked over to the garage and after a bit of cranking got the car to start.

It was quite a car. I had traded my other one for it and I have sneaking suspicion I got worst of the deal. The headlights were about as bright as candle and as for the brakes—well, I'll say they worked after a fashion—but the fashion must have been mighty queer the year that car was made.

The first part of the trip was dull—or as dull as it can be in a car equipped with a young driver who hasn't learned the meaning of fear and who doesn't think bad lights and practically nonexistent brakes are reason enough to reduce speed.

We traveled along, smoking, while I strained my eyes trying to see the road in the feeble glow of the headlights 'til we came to a straight stretch where the road passed over a succession of small hills. I had just reached the top of one of the hills and had started to pick up speed on the way down, when I noticed in the hollow ahead a faint red light. At the top of next hill I saw the headlight an approaching car. Almost without conscious thought I calculated that at the time I reached the small red light the other car would pass me.

Despite all these warnings, I took no notice, thinking the faint red light had been left by a road repair gang and certainly would not impede my progress. Away I went down the hill and near the bottom my speed must have been almost nearly 50 miles an hour. To my horror, I found that the red light was a lamp attached to the back of a huge furniture removal truck, which must have broken down and now blocked half the two-lane country road.

In a flash I knew that if I pulled out to avoid the furniture truck I would have a head-on collision with the oncoming vehicle. I have thought since that I might have pulled off the road and overturned in the ditch but at the time, the knowledge that my brakes were no good crowded out of my mind everything but the two grim alternatives ahead of me.

In a fraction of a second I decided the lesser of the two evils would be to brake as hard as I could and pile into the back the truck. I shouted, "Get down, Bryan!" and at the same time I flung myself under the steering wheel, for I had the sense to know that when we hit, the spokes would be driven straight through my chest.

There was a blinding glare of light, a rushing sound but no crash. I quickly took control of the car again to find that I was rolling down a perfectly clear road. For the next few minutes a deathly hush hung in the car until Bryan said, "You know, Peter, I was praying."

This incident made such an impression on me that a week later I went back over the same stretch of road in daylight and checked the width of it at that spot. I found that it was impossible for a large truck and two cars to pass together at the same time.

I shall never know what happened, because when I let go of the steering wheel the car was headed straight for the rear of the truck about 20 feet ahead. Without human guidance the car must have swerved around the truck, moved through a gap which didn't exist and then straightened itself out again.

Now, 30 years later, the memory of these experiences remains as vivid as if they had happened yesterday . . . and just as vivid in my mind's ear is the rich Irish voice of that motorcyclist, who died too young but lives on in some other plane watching over racy young lads in hopped-up cars—and saving some of them.

THE VOICE FROM NOWHERE

Yves Eriksson
(Dec. 1993)

A saying goes that children should be seen and not heard—but with guardian angels it is most often the other way around, as this letter from a reader illustrates.

M Y FRIEND Bill Chivers and I had spent the day rock climbing in Sequoia National Park, California. Exhausted, we made our way home down the narrow road leading out of the mountains. Bill was driving his VW van down an especially narrow section, with numerous switchbacks and thousand-foot drop-offs. I was in a deep sleep on the passenger side.

Suddenly a voice called, "Wake up now!" I awoke with a start and saw that Bill had fallen asleep. We were about to enter a switchback curve. Another five seconds and we would be hurtling down to certain death. I grabbed the wheel and yelled his name. Awakening, he saw what was happening and wrenched the wheel, barely managing to keep us from going over the side. We were bathed in a rush of adrenaline.

Guardian angel or subconscious awareness, that voice saved our lives.

I HADN'T SAID A WORD— WHO DID?

Suzan L. Wiener
(Dec. 1998)

Here is a final report of an encounter with a guardian angel, where once again the heavenly presence was heard but not seen. From the frequency with which readers tell of being saved from automobile accidents, one might think modern guardian angels constitute a 24/7 heavenly highway patrol.

AFTER my husband Howard and I finally got over a bout of the flu, we decided to take a leisurely drive and stop for lunch at a nice restaurant. All went well, until we started back home. A large truck in front of us was carrying huge pieces of furniture in its bed. It made me nervous; I imagined one of the pieces falling out because the driver was moving at a fast clip. That the furniture wasn't tied down was really surprising, too.

Just as I was about to tell Howard to stay away from the truck, he pulled back automatically. To our horror, we saw a heavy English chair fly out of the bed. It landed just where our car had been. If Howard hadn't pulled back, we would have been seriously injured or killed. Both of us let out a sigh of relief.

Howard was shaken and pulled the car over to the side of the road. I asked him what had made him pull back the way he had. He said he had heard me tell him to. Shocked, I told him I hadn't said a word.

Then I realized it was our Guardian Angel watching over us as she had in the past. It was her voice Howard had heard.

Now we know that we needn't fear the future because our special friend will always be with us.

NOTABLE CONTRIBUTORS

Rosemary Ellen Guiley

Rosemary Ellen Guiley is one of the leading experts in the metaphysical and paranormal fields, with 59 books published including nine single-volume encyclopedias. Her work is translated into 15 languages. Her present work focuses on spiritual growth and development, the afterlife and spirit communications, psychic skills, dreamwork for well-being, working with angels, past and parallel lives, problem hauntings, entity contact experiences, and investigation of unusual paranormal activity. She has done ground-breaking research on Shadow People and the Djinn.

Rosemary is a certified hypnotist through the International Hypnosis Federation. She has studied energy healing, and completed advanced training in bioenergy under Mietek and Margaret Wierkus, Level One Soul Healing under Francesca Szarnicki, and Therapeutic Touch under Dolores Krieger. She is an initiate in Johrei energy healing. She is a reader and teacher of the Tarot, and is co-author with Robert Michael Place of *The Alchemical Tarot* and *The Angels Tarot*. She conducts dreamwork, intuition development, and past-life recall sessions.

Rosemary is a consulting editor of *Fate* magazine, and a board director of the National Museum of Mysteries and Research, a nonprofit educational organization in Columbia, Pennsylvania. She is a past board of director of International Association for the Study of Dreams, and a past member of the board of trustees of the Academy of Religion and Psychical Research (now the Academy for Spiritual and Consciousness Studies). She lives in Connecticut.

Website: www.visionaryliving.com.

John Ronner

John Ronner published his first magazine article at age 15. As a longtime newspaper reporter, he won awards from The Associated Press and other news organizations. Since the mid-1980s, John has spoken with hundreds of people about their experiences with angels. He has discussed his findings in interviews with The Wall Street Journal, Publishers Weekly and other publications and in appearances on such national programs as The Phil Donahue Show, The Learning Channel, Sightings, and the NBC special Angels II. 140,000-plus copies of his books are available in four languages. John's books include Do You Have a Guardian Angel?, The Angels of Cokeville: And Other True Stories of Heavenly Intervention, and Synchronicity: The Mystery of Meaningful Coincidence. His latest book, The Angel Library, a digital edition combining three earlier books, is available from Amazon.com for $2.99 for a download to Kindle readers. See Amazon for a free download of Kindle software for your PC, smart phone or other device.

Website: AngelWatchingMe.com
Blog: TopAngelNews.blogspot.com

Scott Corrales

Scott Corrales became interested in the UFO phenomenon as a result of the heavy UFO activity while he lived in both Mexico and Puerto Rico. He was also influenced by Mexican ufologists, Pedro Ferriz and Salvador Freixedo, a former Jesuit priest who advocated a paranormal, interdimensional interpretation of the phenomenon. In 1990, Scott began translating the works of Freixedo into English, making the literature and research of experts and journalists available to English-reading audiences everywhere. This led to the creation of the SAMIZDAT journal in 1993 and his collaboration with Mexico's CEFP group, Puerto Rico's PRRG, and the foremost researchers of Spain's so-called third generation of UFO researchers.

In 1995, Corrales documented the manifestations of the entity popularly known as the Chupacabras in three works: The Chupacabras Diaries , Nemesis: The Chupacabras at Large , and Chupacabras and Other Mysteries. In 1998, he launched Inexplicata: The Journal of Hispanic Ufology, as the official publication of the nascent Institute of Hispanic Ufology. In addition, Scott has been a guest on numerous radio shows and his articles have been featured in several national publications.

Website: inexplicata.blogspot.com

Leon Thompson

Leon Thompson was a disabled veteran of World War II and a friend of the late Roy Orbison when both men lived in Wink, Texas. He grew up in Wink TX and enlisted in the Army in 1946. He served as a medic in Japan. Upon discharge he returned to Wink and later moved to Washington State where he was employed by the Boeing Co. Later he opened his own art shop in Pike Place Market Leon was an accomplished artist, photographer, collector and published writer and in his earlier years a model. He enjoyed sharing his entertaining history and stories with people.

Brad and Sherry Steiger

Brad Steiger is the author/coauthor of 181 books with over 17 million copies in print. Primarily known for his works on the paranormal and occult, he has also written bestselling biographies of Rudolph Valentino, Judy Garland, Olympic athlete Jim Thorpe, an d Greta Garbo, as well as novels and short stories. Books about the paranormal include *The Gale Encyclopedia [three volumes] of the Unusual and Unexplained, Real Encounters, Different Dimensions, and Otherworldly Beings, Revelation--The Divine Fire. American Indian Medicine Power, Guardian Angels and Spirit Guides, Strangers from the Skies, Real Aliens, Space Beings, and Creatures from Other Worlds, Atlantis Rising,* and *Mysteries of Time and Space,*

His first published articles on the unexplained appeared in 1956, and he has written more than 2,000 articles with paranormal themes. From 1970-'73, his weekly newspaper column, *The Strange World of Brad Steiger,* was carried domestically in over 80 newspapers and overseas from Bombay to Tokyo. He is married to Sherry Steiger, herself the author or coauthor of over 45 books. From the mid-1980s through 2002, they lectured and conducted seminars throughout the United States and overseas.

He is the recipient of many awards and honors including the Genie, for Metaphysical Writer of the Year, the Dani, for Services to Humanity, the Hypnosis Hall of Fame, the Lifetime Achievement Award National UFO and Unexplained Phenomena Conference.

He has appeared on such notable television programs as Nightline, ABC Evening News, with, This Week, Haunted Hollywood,, Inside Edition, and Could It Be a Miracle? San Francisco Chronicle, Chicago Tribune, Publishers Weekly, *FATE,* Parade, and the National Enquirer.

Sherry Steiger is the author/coauthor of *Christmas Miracles, The Teaching Power of Dreams, Divine Intervention, Feats of Incredible Survival, Face to Face with the Unknown, Hollywood and the Supernatural, The Philadelphia Conspiracy and Other UFO Mysteries,* and *Mysteries of Animal Intelligence.*

She is married to Brad Steiger and co-created and produced the highly acclaimed Celebrate Life multi-media awareness program which was performed around the country for colleges, businesses, organizations and churches. For over 30 years, she actively studied the dynamic interaction between the body, mind and spirit in health-related matters as well as the effects of environment and technology on health and wellness. Sherry has addressed audiences and corporate groups from coast to coast. In 1972 Sherry founded one of the earliest nonprofit schools dealing with new approaches to healing and learning, The Butterfly Center for Transformation.

Among Sherry's honors are inclusion in *The World Who's Who of Women, Who's Who among Human Services Professionals, Who's Who in Medicine and Healthcare, International Woman of the Year,* and *Who's Who of Professional and Business Women.*

Sherry worked with a long list of stars for concerts and promotions, including such notables as John Denver, Neil Diamond, the Moody Blues, Lou Rawls, Prince, Melba Moore and many others. As a model, she appeared in such publications as Family Circle, Redbook and Woman's Day. In 1979, Sherry appeared in the highest rated television movie of the year, *Amusement Park* with Mike Connors, Louis Gossett, Jr., Beau Bridges and Martin Landau.

Website www.bradandsherry.com

Melodee K. Currier

Melodee K. Currier writes of herself: I began writing poetry shortly after graduating from high school and wrote off and on for the next several years. My first glimpse that I had writing talent came during a business seminar when I was in my 20's. We were asked to write on a specific topic regarding the workplace. The leader chose my essay to read to the group and said it was the best they had ever seen.

Over the years, I have taken many writing classes, but didn't start to write seriously until I left corporate America in 2008. I started writing paralegal articles and then branched out to a variety of personal essays on a wide variety of subjects. The world of writing is an exciting adventure for me. What will I write about today?

Website: www.melodeecurrier.com

Catherine Ponder

Catherine Ponder is considered one of America's foremost inspirational authors. She has written more than a dozen books, which include such bestsellers as her *Millionaires of the Bible* series. She is a minister of the non-denominational Unity faith, long known as the "pioneer of positive thinking", and heads a global ministry in Palm Desert, California. Catherine wrote her first prosperity book *The Dynamic Laws of Prosperity* in the early 1960's. Her life expanded dramatically whilst she was in the midst of finishing that book.

She has given lectures on the universal principles of prosperity in most of the major cities of America: from Town Hall and the Waldorf Astoria Hotel in New York, to the Phoenix Country Club in Arizona, to the elegant Pioneer Theater Auditorium in Reno, Nevada. From Honolulu to New Orleans she has given interviews on television and radio, as well as numerous interviews by the print media. She is listed in *Who's Who* and the *Social Register,* and has received an honorary doctorate.

Website: catherineponder.wwwhubs.com

Migene Gonzalez-Wippler

Migene González-Wippler was born in Puerto Rico and has degrees in psychology and anthropology from the University of Puerto Rico and from Columbia University. She has worked as a science editor for the Interscience Division of John Wiley, the American Institute of Physics, and the American Museum of Natural History, and as an English editor for the United Nations in Vienna, where she lived for many years. She is a cultural anthropologist and lectures frequently at universities and other educational institutions. She is the noted author of many books on religion and mysticism, including the widely acclaimed *The Keys of the Kingdom/ The Christian Kabbalah, The Complete Book of Spells, Ceremonies & Magic, Dreams and What They Mean to You,* and *What Happens after Death.*

Website: www.migenegonzalezwippler.blog.com

Olga N. Worrall

Olga Worrall was a gifted clairvoyant. She began healing at the age of eight, healing people, animals, and plants. She co-authored several books with her husband, Ambrose Worrall, who was also a notable spiritual healer. They were both founding members of the Spiritual Frontiers Fellowship, a Christian group interested in occult studies. Olga was especially interested in the connection of prayer and meditation in healing. Her books include *Explore Your Psychic World* and *The Gift of Healing.*

Susan Rushing

Susan Rushing writes of herself: I am an intuitive, clairsentient, claircognizant, clairvoyant and psychic medium. My gifts were handed down from psychically gifted and beloved aunts through several generations. My maternal grandfather was a very well-known animal healer in Ross County Ohio, in the foothills of the Appalachian Mountains. From a very young age, I could see and hear things that others could not. These differences led me to seek answers through the study of New Age Spirituality, different holistic healing modalities, energy work, Reiki, Angels, Crystal Therapy and Quantum Healing. I have attained my Reiki Master/Teacher attunement.

I have worked with, and been mentored by some of the top psychics and healers in the United States. Grateful for the gifts of time and love from these professionals, I have come to understand that I am a vessel for Divine Guidance and how readings and energy work are important for personal and spiritual growth, self-love, stress reduction and to learn better spiritual mechanisms to cope and thrive in this physical world. My readings and healing work are done in pure, unconditional love and non-judgment.

Website: susanrushing.com

Susy Smith

Susy Smith was a highly-regarded psychic and the bestselling author of thirty books on parapsychology and survival of consciousness, including *How to Develop Your ESP*, *The Power of the Mind*, and *Life is Forever*. Her many works documenting psychic events and processes brought an unprecedented amount of information to the public view, in simple, easily understandable language.

Boczor Iosif

Boczor Iosif is one of eastern Europe's leading writers on paranormal and unexplained phenomenon. He is internationally known for his writing about the now famous "Object of Aiud" also known as the "Aluminum Wedge of Aiud." This mysterious object is a wedge-shaped piece of aluminum found 2 kilometers east of Aiud, Romania, on the banks of the Mures river in 1974, under thirty-five feet of sand and alongside two mastodon bones. Taken to the Archeological Institute of Cluj-Napoca for examination, where it was determined to be made of aluminum alloy encased in a layer of oxide no less than a millimeter thick, which is said to indicate an age of at least 300 to 400 years.

Made in the USA
Middletown, DE
16 April 2016